THE LANDSCAPE OF HISTORY

ALSO BY JOHN LEWIS GADDIS

The United States and the Origins of the Cold War, 1941–1947

Russia, the Soviet Union, and the United States: An Interpretive History

Strategies of Containment: A Critical Appraisal of Postwar American National Security Policy

The Long Peace: Inquiries into the History of the Cold War

The United States and the End of the Cold War: Implications, Reconsiderations, Provocations

We Now Know: Rethinking Cold War History

THE LANDSCAPE OF HISTORY

How Historians Map the Past

JOHN LEWIS GADDIS

OXFORD
UNIVERSITY PRESS

OXFORD
UNIVERSITY PRESS

Oxford New York
Auckland   Bangkok   Buenos Aires   Cape Town   Chennai
Dar es Salaam   Delhi   Hong Kong   Istanbul   Karachi   Kolkata
Kuala Lumpur   Madrid   Melbourne   Mexico City   Mumbai   Nairobi
São Paulo   Shanghai   Taipei   Tokyo   Toronto

First published by Oxford University Press, Inc., 2002
First issued as an Oxford University Press paperback, 2004
198 Madison Avenue, New York, New York 10016
www.oup.com

Oxford is a registered trademark of Oxford University Press

Library of Congress Cataloging-in-Publication Data
Gaddis, John Lewis.
The landscape of history : how historians map the past / John Lewis Gaddis.
p. cm. Includes index.
ISBN-13 978-0-19-517157-0 (PBK.)
1. History—Philosophy. 2. History—Methodology.
3. Aesthetics—History. I. Title.
D16.8 .G23 2002   901—dc21   2002010392

Book design and composition by Mark McGarry, Texas Type & Book Works.
Set in Linotype Fairfield.

9 8 7 6

Printed in the United States of America

For Toni

The Love of Life and a Life of Love

CONTENTS

CONTENTS

PREFACE

THE UNIVERSITY OF OXFORD has again provided a hospitable setting in which to write a book. The occasion this time was the 2000/1
George Eastman Visiting Professorship in Balliol College, a chair dat-
ing back to 1929 whose occupants have included Felix Frankfurter,
Linus Pauling, Willard Quine, George F. Kennan, Lionel Trilling, Clif-
ford Geertz, William H. McNeill, Natalie Zemon Davis, and Robin
Winks. As befits a position with such diverse and distinguished predecessors, the Eastman electors do not find it necessary to provide current chairholders with detailed instructions as to what they are
expected to do. My own letter of appointment specified only "partici-
pation in twenty-four academic functions during the three terms of
the academic year." It then added, accurately enough as I discovered,
"that the Eastman Professor enjoys considerable scope for flexibility in
adjusting the pedagogical activities in combination with scholarly projects which the holder may wish to pursue."

Confronted with so much latitude in so congenial a setting, I was
at first at a loss to know how to use my time. One possibility, I sup-
pose, would have been simply to dine: high table at Oxford is definitely an "academic function." Another would have been to spend the

year doing research, but this would have disappointed my hosts, who
clearly expected some sort of visibility. A third would have been to lecture on Cold War history; but I'd done that as Harmsworth Professor
eight years earlier and had since published the lectures.[1] Even in a
rapidly changing field like this one, would there be that much new to
say? I rather doubted it.

So in the end, I settled on something completely different: a set of
lectures, delivered as before in the Examination Schools building on
High Street, on the admittedly ambitious subject of how historians
think. I had several purposes in mind in undertaking this project, the
first of which was to pay homage to scholars now dead and to students
very much alive, both of whom had taught me. The scholars, in particular, were Marc Bloch and E. H. Carr, whose respective introductions
to the historical method, *The Historian's Craft* and *What Is History?*,
first forced me to think about what historians do. The students were
my own, undergraduates and graduates at Ohio, Yale, and Oxford uni-
versities, with whom I'd spent a good deal of time discussing these
and other less familiar works on historical methodology.

A second purpose derived from the first. I'd begun to worry that all
this reading and talking might soon begin to produce, in my own mind,
something like the effect Cervantes describes when a certain man of
La Mancha read too many books on knight-errantry: "he so bewildered
himself in this kind of study that . . . his brain . . . dried up, [and] he
came at last to lose his wits."[2] I felt the need, at this stage in life, to
begin to sort things out, lest I start attacking windmills. It's possible, of
course, that I've already arrived at that stage, and that these lectures
were the first offensive—but I'll leave that for my readers to judge.

My third purpose—whether or not I'd dodged the dangers implied
in the second—was to do some updating. A lot has happened since
the Nazis executed Bloch in 1944, leaving us with a classic that breaks
off, like Thucydides, in mid-sentence; and since the more fortunate
Carr completed his George Macaulay Trevelyan lectures, which
became his classic, at Cambridge in 1961. It's my impression, though,

that it's not so much they as we who need the updating. For Bloch and Carr anticipated certain developments in the physical and biological sciences that have brought those disciplines closer than they once were to what historians had been doing all along. Most social scientists have hardly noticed these trends, and most historians, even as they read and teach Bloch and Carr, neglect what these authors were suggesting about a convergence of the historical method with those of the so-called "hard" sciences.[3]

That suggests my fourth purpose, which was to encourage my fellow historians to make their methods more explicit. We normally resist doing this. We work within a wide variety of styles, but we prefer in all of them that form conceal function. We recoil from the notion that our writing should replicate, say, the design of the Pompidou Center in Paris, which proudly places its escalators, plumbing, wiring, and ductwork on the *outside* of the building, so that they're there for all to see. We don't question the need for such structures, only the impulse to exhibit them. Our reluctance to reveal our own, however, too often confuses our students—even, at times, ourselves—as to just what it is we do.

Bloch and Carr had little patience with such methodological modesty,[4] and that brings me to my final purpose, which has to do with teaching. It's striking that, with all the time that's passed since their introductions to the historical method came out, no better ones for use in the classroom have yet appeared.[5] The reason is not just that Bloch and Carr were accomplished methodologists: we've had many since and some more skilled. What distinguished them was the clarity, brevity, and wit— in a word, the elegance—with which they expressed themselves. They showed that you can discuss ductwork gracefully. Few methodologists attempt this today, which is why they speak mostly to themselves and not to the rest of us. I'm sure it's quixotic, on my part, even to aspire to the example of these two great predecessors. But I should like at least to try.

It remains only to thank the people who made this project possible:

Adam Roberts, who kindly suggested a return visit to Oxford eight years ago as I was completing my first; the Association of American Rhodes Scholars, for supporting the Eastman Professorship and for providing such comfortable lodgings in Eastman House; the master and fellows of Balliol College, who in so many ways made my wife Toni and me feel welcome there; the students, faculty, and friends who attended my lectures, and who provided so many insightful comments on them in the question period afterwards; my indefatigable Yale research assistant Ryan Floyd; and, finally, several careful and critical readers of these chapters in draft form, especially India Cooper, Toni Dorfman, Michael Frame, Michael Gaddis, Alexander George, Peter Ginna, Lorenz Lüthi, William H. McNeill, Ian Shapiro, and Jeremi Suri. I should also like to thank the Oxford microbes, which were much more manageable than they had been eight years earlier.

Portions of what follows have appeared elsewhere, in "The Tragedy of Cold War History," *Diplomatic History* 17 (Winter 1993), 1–16; *On Contemporary History: An Inaugural Lecture Delivered before the University of Oxford on 18 May 1993* (Oxford: Clarendon Press, 1995); "History, Science, and the Study of International Relations," in *Explaining International Relations since 1945*, ed. Ngaire Woods (New York: Oxford University Press, 1996), pp. 32–48; "History, Theory, and Common Ground," *International Security* 22 (Summer 1997), 75–85; "On the Interdependency of Variables; or, How Historians Think," *Whitney Humanities Center Newsletter*, Yale University, February 1999; and "In Defense of Particular Generalization: Rewriting Cold War History," in *Bridges and Boundaries: Historians, Political Scientists, and the Study of International Relations*, ed. Colin Elman and Miriam Fendius Elman (Cambridge, Mass.: MIT Press, 2001), pp. 301–26. The overall argument, I hope and trust though, is a new one.

The dedication, this time, can only go to the person who changed my life.

NEW HAVEN
APRIL 2002

THE LANDSCAPE OF HISTORY

Caspar David Friedrich, *The Wanderer above the Sea of Fog*
(c. 1818. Hamburg Kunsthalle, Hamburg, Germany /
Bridgman Art Library.)

Chapter One

THE LANDSCAPE OF HISTORY

A YOUNG MAN STANDS hatless in a black coat on a high rocky point. His back is turned toward us, and he is bracing himself with a walking stick against the wind that blows his hair in tangles. Before him lies a fog-shrouded landscape in which the fantastic shapes of more distant promontories are only partly visible. The far horizon reveals mountains off to the left, plains to the right, and perhaps very far away—one can't be sure—an ocean. But maybe it's just more fog, merging imperceptibly into clouds. The painting, which dates from 1818, is a familiar one: Caspar David Friedrich's *The Wanderer above a Sea of Fog*. The impression it leaves is contradictory, suggesting at once mastery over a landscape and the insignificance of an individual within it. We see no face, so it's impossible to know whether the prospect confronting the young man is exhilarating, or terrifying, or both.

Paul Johnson used Friedrich's painting some years ago as the cover for his book *The Birth of the Modern*, to evoke the rise of romanticism and the advent of the industrial revolution.[1] I should like to use it here to summon up something more personal, which is my own sense— admittedly idiosyncratic—of what historical consciousness is all about. The logic of beginning with a landscape may not be immediately obvious. But consider the power of metaphor, on the one hand, and the particular combination of economy and intensity with which visual images can express metaphors, on the other.

The best introduction I know to the scientific method, John Ziman's *Reliable Knowledge: An Exploration of the Grounds for Belief in Science*, points out that scientific insights often arise from such realizations as "that the behavior of an electron in an atom is 'like' the vibration of air in a spherical container, or that the random configuration of the long chain of atoms in a polymer molecule is 'like' the motion of a drunkard across a village green."[2] "Reality is still to be embraced and reported without flinching," the sociobiologist Edward O. Wilson has added. "But it is also best delivered the same way it was discovered, retaining a comparable vividness and play of the emotions."[3] It's here, I think, that science, history, and art have something in common: they all depend on metaphor, on the recognition of patterns, on the realization that something is "like" something else.

For me, the posture of Friedrich's wanderer—this striking image of a back turned toward the artist and all who have since seen his work— is "like" that of historians. Most of us consider it our business, after all, to turn our back on wherever it is we may be going, and to focus our attention, from whatever vantage point we can find, on where we've been. We pride ourselves on *not* trying to predict the future, as our colleagues in economics, sociology, and political science attempt to do. We resist letting contemporary concerns influence us—the term "presentism," among historians, is no compliment. We advance bravely into the future with our eyes fixed firmly on the past: the image we present to the world is, to put it bluntly, that of a rear end.[4]

I.

Historians do, to be sure, assume *some* things about what's to come. It's a good bet, for example, that time will continue to pass, that gravity will continue to extend itself through space, and that Michaelmas term at Oxford will continue to be, as it has been for well over seven hundred years, dreary, dark, and damp. But we know these things about the future only from having learned about the past: without it we'd have no sense of even these fundamental truths, to say nothing of the words with which to express them, or even of who or where or what we are. We know the future only by the past we project into it. History, in this sense, is all we have.

But the past, in another sense, is something we can never have. For by the time we've become aware of what has happened it's already inaccessible to us: we cannot relive, retrieve, or rerun it as we might some laboratory experiment or computer simulation. We can only *represent* it. We can portray the past as a near or distant landscape, much as Friedrich has depicted what his wanderer sees from his lofty perch. We can perceive shapes through the fog and mist, we can speculate as to their significance, and sometimes we can even agree among ourselves as to what these are. Barring the invention of a time machine, though, we can never go back there to see for sure.

Science fiction, of course, has invented time machines. Indeed two recent novels, Connie Willis's *Doomsday Book* and Michael Crichton's *Timelines*, feature graduate students in history at, respectively, Oxford and Yale, who use these devices to project themselves back to England and France in the fourteenth century for the purpose of researching their dissertations.[5] Both authors suggest some things time travel might do for us. It could, for example, give us a "feel" for a particular time and place: the novels evoke the denser forests, clearer air, and much louder singing birds of medieval Europe, as well as the muddy roads, rotting food, and smelly people. What they don't show is that we could easily detect the larger patterns of a period by visiting it, because the characters keep getting caught up in complications of everyday life that tend to limit perspective. Like catching the plague, or being burned at the stake, or getting their heads chopped off.

Maybe this is just what it takes to keep the novel exciting, or to make the movie rights marketable. I'm inclined to think, though, that there's a larger point lurking here: it is that the direct experience of events isn't necessarily the best path toward understanding them, because your field of vision extends no further than your own immediate senses. You lack the capacity, when trying to figure out how to survive a famine, or flee a band of brigands, or fight from within a suit of armor, to function as a historian might do. You're not likely to take the time to contrast conditions in fourteenth-century France with those under Charlemagne or the Romans, or to compare what might have been parallels in Ming China or pre-Columbian Peru. Because the individual is "narrowly restricted by his senses and power of concentration," Marc Bloch writes in *The Historian's Craft*, he "never perceives more than a tiny patch of the vast tapestry of events. . . . In this respect, the student of the present is scarcely any better off than the historian of the past."[6]

I'd argue, indeed, that the historian of the past is *much better off* than the participant in the present, from the simple fact of having an expanded horizon. Gertrude Stein got close to the reason in her brief 1938 biography of Picasso: "When I was in America I for the first time travelled pretty much all the time in an airplane and when I looked at the earth I saw all the lines of cubism made at a time when not any painter had ever gone up in an airplane. I saw there on earth the mingling lines of Picasso, coming and going, developing and destroying themselves."[7] What was happening here, quite literally, was detachment from, and consequent elevation above, a landscape: a departure from the normal that provided a new perception of what was real. It was what the Montgolfier brothers saw from their balloon over Paris in 1783, or the Wright brothers from their first "Flyer" in 1903, or the Apollo astronauts when they flew around the moon at Christmas 1968, thus becoming the first humans to view the earth set against the darkness of space. It's also, of course, what Friedrich's wanderer sees from his mountaintop, as have countless others for whom elevation, by shifting perspective, has enlarged experience.

This brings us around, then, to one of the things historians do. For if you think of the past as a landscape, then history is the way we represent it, and it's that act of representation that lifts us above the familiar to let us experience vicariously what we can't experience directly: a wider view.

II.

What, though, do we gain from such a view? Several things, I think, the first of which is a sense of identity that parallels the process of growing up. Taking off in an airplane makes you feel both large and small at the same time. You can't help but have a sense of mastery as your airline of choice detaches you from the ground, lifts you above the traffic jams surrounding the airport, and reveals vast horizons stretching out beyond it—assuming, of course, that you have a window seat, it isn't a cloudy day, and you aren't one of those people whose fear of flying causes them to keep their eyes clamped shut from takeoff to landing. But as you gain altitude, you also can't help noticing how small you are in relation to the landscape that lies before you. The experience is at once exhilarating and terrifying.

So is life. We are born, each of us, with such self-centeredness that only the fact of being babies, and therefore cute, saves us. Growing up is largely a matter of growing out of that condition: we soak in impressions, and as we do so we dethrone ourselves—or at least most of us do—from our original position at the center of the universe. It's like taking off in an airplane: the establishment of identity requires recognizing our relative insignificance in the larger scheme of things. Remember how it felt to have your parents unexpectedly produce a younger sibling, or abandon you to the tender mercies of kindergarten? Or what it was like to enter your first public or private school, or to arrive at places like Oxford, or Yale, or the Hogwarts School of Witchcraft and Wizardry?[8] Or as a teacher to confront your first classroom filled with sullen, squirmy, slumbering, solipsistic students? Just as you've cleared one hurdle another is set before you. Each event diminishes your authority at just the moment at which you think you've become an authority.

If that's what maturity means in human relationships—the arrival at identity by way of insignificance—then I would define historical consciousness as the projection of that maturity through time. We understand how much has preceded us, and how unimportant we are in relation to it. We learn our place, and we come to realize that it isn't a large one. "Even a superficial acquaintance with the existence, through millennia of time, of numberless human beings," the historian Geoffrey Elton has pointed out, "helps to correct the normal adolescent inclination to relate the world to oneself instead of relating oneself to the world." History teaches "those adjustments and insights which help the adolescent to become adult, surely a worthy service in the education of youth."[9] Mark Twain put it even better:

> That it took a hundred million years to prepare the world for [man] is proof that that is what it was done for. I suppose it is. I dunno. If the Eiffel Tower were now representing the world's age, the skin of paint on the pinnacle knob at its summit would represent man's share of that age; and anybody would perceive that the skin was what the tower was built for. I reckon they would, I dunno.[10]

Here too, though, there's a paradox, for although the discovery of geologic or "deep" time diminished the significance of human beings in the overall history of the universe, it also, in the eyes of Charles Darwin, T. H. Huxley, Mark Twain, and many others, dethroned God from *his* position at its center—which left no one else around but man.[11] The recognition of human insignificance did not, as one might have expected, enhance the role of divine agency in explaining human affairs: it had just the opposite effect. It gave rise to a secular consciousness that, for better or for worse, placed the responsibility for what happens in history squarely on the people who live through history.

What I'm suggesting, therefore, is that just as historical consciousness demands detachment from—or if you prefer, elevation above—the landscape that is the past, so it also requires a certain displacement: an ability to shift back and forth between humility and mastery. Niccolò Machiavelli made the point precisely in his famous preface to *The Prince*: how was it, he asked his patron Lorenzo de' Medici, that "a man from a low and mean state dares to discuss and give rules for the governments of princes?" Being Machiavelli, he then answered his own question:

> For just as those who sketch landscapes place themselves down in
> the plain to consider the nature of mountains and high places and
> to consider the nature of low places place themselves high atop
> mountains, similarly to know well the nature of peoples one needs
> to be [a] prince, and to know well the nature of princes one needs
> to be of the people.[12]

You feel small, whether as a courtier or an artist or a historian, because you recognize your insignificance in an infinite universe. You know you can never yourself rule a kingdom, or capture on canvas everything you see on a distant horizon, or recapture in your books and lectures everything that's happened in even the most particular part of the past. The best you can do, whether with a prince or a landscape or the past, is to *represent* reality: to smooth over the details, to look for larger patterns, to consider how you can use what you see for your own purposes.

That very act of representation, though, makes you feel large, because you yourself are in charge of the representation: it's you who must make complexity comprehensible, first to yourself, then to others. And the power that resides in representation can be great indeed, as Machiavelli certainly understood. For how much influence today does Lorenzo de' Medici have, compared to the man who applied to be his tutor?

Historical consciousness therefore leaves you, as does maturity itself, with a simultaneous sense of your own significance and insignificance. Like Friedrich's wanderer, you dominate a landscape even as you're diminished by it. You're suspended between sensibilities that are at odds with one another; but it's precisely within that suspension that your own identity—whether as a person or a historian—tends to reside. Self-doubt must always precede self-confidence. It should never, however, cease to accompany, challenge, and by these means discipline self-confidence.

III.

Machiavelli, who so strikingly combined both qualities, wrote *The Prince*, as he immodestly informed Lorenzo de' Medici, "considering that no greater gift could be made by me than to give you the capacity to be able to understand in a very short time all that I have learned and understood in so many years and with so many hardships and dangers for myself." The purpose of his representation was *distillation*: he sought to "package" a large body of information into a compact usable form so that his patron could quickly master it. It's no accident that the book is a short one. What Machiavelli offered was a compression of historical experience that would vicariously enlarge personal experience. "For since men almost always walk on paths beaten by others . . . , a prudent man should always . . . imitate those who have been most excellent, so that if his own virtue does not reach that far, it is at least in the odor of it."[13]

This is as good a summary of the uses of historical consciousness as I have found. I like it because it makes two points: first, that we're bound to learn from the past whether or not we make the effort, since it's the only data base we have; and second, that we might as well try to do so systematically. E. H. Carr elaborated on the first of these arguments when he observed, in *What Is History?*, that the size and reasoning capacity of the human brain are probably no greater now than they were five thousand years ago, but that very few human beings live now as they did then. The effectiveness of human thinking, he continued, "has been multiplied many times by learning and incorporating . . . the experience of the intervening generations." The inheritance of acquired characteristics may not work in biology, but it does in human affairs: "History is progress through the transmission of acquired skills from one generation to another."[14]

As his biographer Jonathan Haslam has pointed out, Carr's idea of "progress" in twentieth-century history tended disconcertingly to associate that quality with the accumulation of power in the hands of the state.[15] But in *What Is History?* Carr was making a larger and less controversial argument: that if we can widen the range of experience beyond what we as individuals have encountered, if we can draw upon the experiences of others who've had to confront comparable situations in the past, then—although there are no guarantees—our *chances* of acting wisely should increase proportionally.

This brings us to Machiavelli's second point, which is that we should learn from the past systematically. Historians ought not to delude themselves into thinking that they provide the *only* means by which acquired skills—and ideas—are transmitted from one generation to the next. Culture, religion, technology, environment, and tradition can all do this. But history is arguably the best method of enlarging experience in such a way as to command the widest possible consensus on what the significance of that experience might be.[16]

I know that statement will raise eyebrows, because historians so often and so visibly disagree with one another. We relish revisionism and distrust orthodoxy, not least because were we to do otherwise, we might put ourselves out of business. We have, in recent years, embraced postmodernist insights about the relative character of all historical judgments—the inseparability of the observer from that which is being observed—although some of us feel that we've known this all along.[17] Historians appear, in short, to have only squishy ground upon which to stand, and hence little basis for claiming any consensus at all on what the past might tell us with respect to the present and future.

Except when you ask the question: compared to what? No other mode of inquiry comes any closer to producing such a consensus, and most fall far short of it. The very fact that orthodoxies so dominate the realms of religion and culture suggests the absence of agreement from below, and hence the need to impose it from above. People adapt to technology and environment in so many different ways as to defy generalization. Traditions manifest themselves so variously across such diverse institutions and cultures that they provide hardly any consistency on what the past should signify. The historical method, in this sense, beats all the others.

Nor does it demand agreement, among its practitioners, as to precisely what the "lessons" of history are: a consensus can incorporate contradictions. It's part of growing up to learn that there are competing versions of truth, and that you yourself must choose which to embrace. It's part of historical consciousness to learn the same thing: that there is no "correct" interpretation of the past, but that the act of interpreting is itself a vicarious enlargement of experience from which you can benefit. It would ill serve any prince to be told that the past offers simple lessons—or even, for some situations, any lessons at all. "The prince can gain the people to himself in many modes," Machiavelli wrote at one point, "for which one cannot give certain rules because the modes vary according to circumstances." The general proposition still holds, though, that "for a prince it is necessary to have the people friendly; otherwise he has no remedy in adversity."[18]

This gets us close to what historians do—or at least, to echo Machiavelli, should have the odor of doing: it is to interpret the past for the purposes of the present with a view to managing the future, but to do so without suspending the capacity to assess the particular circumstances in which one might have to act, or the relevance of past actions to them. To accumulate experience is not to endorse its automatic application, for part of historical consciousness is the ability to see differences as well as similarities, to understand that generalizations do not always hold in particular circumstances.

That sounds pretty daunting—until you consider another arena of human activity in which this distinction between the general and the particular is so ubiquitous that we hardly even think about it: it's the wide world of sports. To achieve proficiency in basketball, baseball, or even bridge, you have to know the rules of the game, and you have to practice. But these rules, together with what your coach can teach you about applying them, are nothing more than a distillation of accumulated experience: they serve the same function that Machiavelli intended *The Prince* to serve for Lorenzo de' Medici. They're generalizations: compressions and distillations of the past in order to make it usable in the future.

Each game you play, however, will have its own characteristics: the skill of your opponent, the adequacy of your own preparation, the circumstances in which the competition takes place. No competent coach would lay out a plan to be mechanically followed throughout the game: you have to leave a lot to the discretion—and the good judgment—of the individual players. The fascination of sports resides in the intersection of the general with the particular. The practice of life is much the same.

Studying the past is no sure guide to predicting the future. What it does do, though, is to *prepare* you for the future by expanding experience, so that you can increase your skills, your stamina—and, if all goes well, your wisdom. For while it may be true, as Machiavelli estimated, "that fortune is the arbiter of half our actions," it's also the case that "she leaves the other half, or close to it, for us to govern." Or, as he also put it, "God does not want to do everything."[19]

IV.

Just how, though, do you present historical experience for the purpose of enlarging personal experience? To include too little information can render the whole exercise irrelevant. To include too much can overload the circuits and crash the system. The historian has got to strike a balance, and that means recognizing a trade-off between literal and abstract representation. Let me illustrate this with two well-known artistic portrayals of the same subject.

The first is Jan van Eyck's great double portrait *The Marriage of Giovanni Arnolfini*, from 1434, which documents a relationship between a man and a woman in such precise detail that we can see

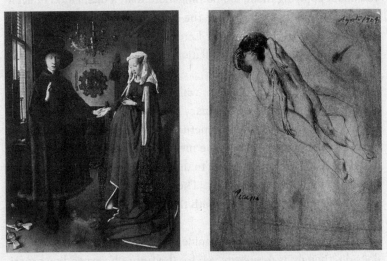

Two representations of the same subject,
one from a particular time and the other for all time.
Jan van Eyck, *The Marriage of Giovanni Arnolfini*, 1434,
London, National Gallery (Alinari / Art Resource, New York), and Pablo
Picasso, *The Lovers*, 1904, Musée Picasso, Paris (Réunion des Musées
Nationaux / Art Resource, New York; © 2002 Estate of Pablo Picasso /
Artists Rights Society (ARS), New York).

every fold in their clothes, every frill in the lace, the apples on the windowsill, the shoes on the floor, the individual hairs on the little dog, and even the artist himself reflected in the mirror. The picture is striking because it's as close as anything we have to photographic realism four hundred years before photography was invented. This can only have been 1434, these can only have been the Arnolfinis, and they can only have been painted in Bruges. We get the vicarious experience of a distant but very particular time and place.

Now, contrast this with Picasso's *The Lovers*, an ink, watercolor, and charcoal drawing dashed off quickly in 1904. The image, like van Eyck's, leaves little doubt as to the subject. But here everything has been stripped away: background, furnishings, shoes, dog, even clothes, and we're down to the essence of the matter. What we have is a transmission of vicarious experience so generic that anyone from Adam and Eve onward would immediately understand it. The very point of this drawing is the abstraction that flows from its absence of context, and it's this that projects it so effectively across time and space.

Switch now, if you can manage this leap, to Thucydides, in whom I find both the particularity of a van Eyck and the generality of a Picasso. He is, at times, so photographic in his narrative that he could be writing a modern screenplay. He tells us, for example, of a Plataean attempt against a Peloponnesian wall in which the soldiers advanced with only their left feet shod to keep from slipping in the mud, and in which the inadvertent dislodgment of a single roof tile raised the alarm. He places us in the middle of the Athenian attack on Pylos in 425 B.C. just as precisely as those remarkable first moments of Steven Spielberg's film *Saving Private Ryan* place us on the Normandy beaches in 1944 A.D. He makes us hear the sick and wounded Athenians on Sicily "loudly calling to each individual comrade or relative whom they could see, hanging upon the necks of their tent-fellows in the act of departure, and following as far as they could, and when their bodily strength failed them, calling again and again upon heaven and shrieking aloud as they were left behind."[20] There is, in short, an authenticity in this particularity that puts us there at least as effectively as one of Michael Crichton's time machines.

But Thucydides, unlike Crichton, is also a great generalizer. He meant his work, he tells us, for those inquirers "who desire an exact knowledge of the past as an aid to the interpretation of the future, which in the course of human things must resemble if it does not reflect it." He knew that abstraction—we might even call it a Picasso-like separation from context—is what makes generalizations hold up over time. Hence he has the Athenians telling the rebellious Melians, as a timeless principle, that "the strong do what they can and the weak suffer what they must": it follows that the Athenians "put to death all the grown men whom they took, and sold the women and children for slaves, and subsequently sent out five hundred colonists and inhabited the place themselves." Thucydides also shows us, though, that there are exceptions to any rule: when the Mityleneans rebel and the Athenians conquer them, the strong suddenly have second thoughts and send out a second ship to overtake the first, countermanding the order to slaughter or enslave the weak.[21]

This tension between particularization and generalization—between literal and abstract representation—comes with the territory, I think, when you're transmitting vicarious experience. A simple chronicle of details, however graphic, locks you into a particular time and place. You move beyond it by abstracting, but abstracting is an artificial exercise, involving an oversimplification of complex realities. It's analogous to what happened in the world of art once it began, in the late nineteenth century, to depart from the literal representation of reality. One objective of impressionism, cubism, and futurism was to find a way to represent motion from within the necessarily static media of paint, canvas, and frame. Abstraction arose as a form of liberation, a new view of reality that suggested something of the flow of time.[22] It worked, though, only by distorting space.

Historians, in contrast, employ abstraction to overcome a different constraint, which is their separation in time from their subjects.

Artists coexist with the objects they're representing, which means that it's always possible for them to shift the view, adjust the light, or move the model.[23] Historians can't do this: because what they represent is in the past, they can never alter it. But they can, by that means of the particular form of abstraction we know as *narrative*, portray movement through time, something an artist can only hint at.

There's always a balance to be struck, though, for the more time the narrative covers, the less detail it can provide. It's like the Heisenberg uncertainty principle, in which the precise measurement of one variable renders another one imprecise.[24] This then, is yet another of the polarities involved in historical consciousness: the tension between the literal and the abstract, between the detailed depiction of what lies at some point in the past, on the one hand, and the sweeping sketch of what extends over long stretches of it, on the other.

V.

Which brings me back to Friedrich's *Wanderer*, a representation in art that comes close to suggesting visually what historical consciousness is all about. The back turned toward us. Elevation from, not immersion in, a distant landscape. The tension between significance and insignificance, the way you feel both large and small at the same time. The polarities of generalization and particularization, the gap between abstract and literal representation. But there's something else here as well: a sense of curiosity mixed with awe mixed with a determination to find things out—to penetrate the fog, to distill experience, to *depict* reality—that is as much an artistic vision as a scientific sensibility.

Harold Bloom has written of Shakespeare that he created our concept of ourselves by discovering ways—never before achieved—of portraying human nature on the stage.[25] John Madden's film *Shakespeare in Love*, I think, shows that actually happening: it's the moment when *Romeo and Juliet* has been staged for the first time, when the last lines have been delivered, and when the audience, utterly amazed, sits silently with eyes bulging and mouths agape, unsure of what to do. Confronting uncharted territory, whether in theater, history, or human affairs, produces something like that sense of wonder. Which is probably why *Shakespeare in Love* ends at the beginning of *Twelfth Night,* with Viola shipwrecked on an uncharted continent, filled with dangers but also with infinite possibilities. And as in Friedrich's *Wanderer,* it's a backside we see in that last long shot as she wades ashore.

Now, I don't mean to suggest that historians can, with any credibility, play the role of Gwyneth Paltrow. We're supposed to be solid, dispassionate chroniclers of events, not given to allowing our emotions and our intuitions to affect what we do, or so we've traditionally been taught. I worry, though, that if we don't allow for these things, and for the sense of excitement and wonder they bring to the doing of history, then we're missing much of what the field is all about. The first lines Shakespeare has Viola speak, filled as they are with intelligence, curiosity, and some dread, could well be the starting point for any historian contemplating the landscape of history: "What country, friends, is this?"

Chapter Two

TIME AND SPACE

ONE OF THE THINGS that's striking about that final scene in *Shakespeare in Love* is its suggestion of an abundance of time and space: all possibilities are open; nothing is ruled out. "Had we but world enough and time," the poet Andrew Marvell wrote regretfully, acknowledging that he did not.[1] But in this cinematic image of a backside, an empty beach, and an uncharted continent, it seems that we really do.

Individual historians, like Marvell, are of course bound by time and space, but history as a discipline isn't. Precisely because of their detachment from and elevation above the landscape of the past, historians are able to manipulate time and space in ways they could never manage as normal people. They can compress these dimensions, expand them, compare them, measure them, even transcend them, almost as poets, playwrights, novelists, and film-makers do. Historians have always been, in this sense, abstractionists: the literal representation of reality is not their task.

And yet they must accomplish these manipulations in such a way as at least to approach the standards for verification that exist within the social, physical, and biological sciences. Artists don't normally expect to have their sources checked. Historians do.[2] That fact suspends us somewhere in between the arts and the sciences: we feel free to rise above the constraints of time and space, to use our imagination, to boldly go—as the scriptwriters of *Star Trek* might have put it in their relentless pursuit of the split infinitive—where no actual person has or ever could have gone before. But we have to do this in such a way as to convince our students, our colleagues, and anyone else who reads our work that these departures from the dimensions in which we usually live our lives do indeed give us reliable information about how people in the past lived theirs. This isn't an easy task.

I.

Let me begin my discussion of it with one of the most famous of all fictional rearrangements of time and space (to say nothing of gender), Virginia Woolf's novel *Orlando*. It begins and ends with her eponymous hero sitting quietly on a hill, under a large oak tree, from which he (who by the end of the book has become a she) can see some thirty English counties, "or forty, perhaps, if the weather was very fine." The spires and smoke of London are visible in one direction, the English Channel in another, and the "craggy top and serrated edges of Snowden [*sic*]" in another. Orlando returns to this place regularly over some three and a half centuries without visibly aging. Elizabeth I finds him enchanting, but she—for there is an unexpected change of sex about a third of the way through—is still flourishing in the reign of George V. So what's going on here?

Well, first of all, Orlando is a thinly disguised portrayal of Woolf's lover, Vita Sackville-West: what better gift than to liberate such a person from constraints of time, space, and gender? But the novel is also Woolf's send-up of biography as a genre—especially those tedious multivolume "life and times" monuments favored by the Victorians.[3]

"It was now November," she tells us in recounting one of the less eventful years in Orlando's life:

> After November, comes December. Then January, February, March, and April. After April comes May. June, July, August follow. Next is September. Then October, and so, behold, here we are back at November again, with a whole year accomplished. This method of writing biography, though it has its merits, is a little bare, perhaps, and the reader, if we go on with it, may complain that he could recite the calendar for himself and so save his pocket whatever sum the publisher may think it proper to charge for the book.

More significantly for our purposes, and as this quote suggests, *Orlando* is a protest against the literal representation of reality. Woolf makes the point most clearly in a striking passage on the nature of time: "An hour, once it lodges in the queer element of the human spirit, may be stretched to fifty or a hundred times its clock length; on the other hand, an hour may be accurately represented on the time-piece of the mind by one second. This extraordinary discrepancy between time on the clock and time in the mind is less known than it should be, and deserves fuller investigation."[4]

So let us take her up on that suggestion, and see where it leads. The desk calendar method of writing history has ancient precedents in the form of chronicles, which dutifully recount the weather, the crops, and the phases of the moon, as well as more extraordinary developments. But as the philosopher of history Hayden White has noted, events recorded in the strict order of their occurrence almost immediately get rearranged into a story with a discrete beginning, middle, and end.[5] These then become histories, and White's analysis of them beyond this point becomes jargon-laden. Suffice it to say, though, that when he's writing about "emplotment" and "formist, organicist, mechanistic, and contextualist" modes of explanation, what he's really describing is the historian's liberation from the limitations of time and space: the freedom to give greater attention to some things than to others and thus to depart from strict chronology; the license to connect things disconnected in space, and thus to rearrange geography.

These procedures are so basic that historians tend to take them for granted: we rarely even think about what we're doing when we do it. And yet they get at the heart of what we mean by representation, which is simply the rearrangement of reality to suit our purposes.[6] As a way of illustrating this point, consider Thomas Babington Macaulay and Henry Adams, two prominent nineteenth-century exemplars of the traditional historical narrative. Despite their reputations, both managed to liberate themselves from literal representation with a self-confidence that would have astonished the world of art at the time, had they been capable of expressing it in visual terms.

The multiple volumes of Macaulay's *History of England*, published between 1848 and 1861, and of Adams's *History of the United States of America during the Administrations of Thomas Jefferson and James Madison*, which appeared between 1889 and 1891, move grandly through time, not hesitating to select evidence that confirms their authors' convictions and to neglect that which does not. Macaulay, hence, imposes the "Whig" interpretation of history so authoritatively that subsequent generations of historians have staggered under its weight. Adams, for his part, bears the burden of family history: his view of Jefferson and Madison is, inescapably—even genetically— that of John and John Quincy Adams.[7] The discrepancy Woolf detected between time on the clock and time in the mind is, in this filtering of evidence, most assuredly there.

But Macaulay and Adams do not *only* move through time: they both begin their histories with a trip through space at a single point in time that bears a striking resemblance to that of Orlando from his or her oak tree. Macaulay's famous third chapter on "The State of England in 1685" views the entire country as no actual observer could possibly have done.[8] We see things from a distance, to be sure, as when he tells us that we might recognize "Snowdon and Windermere, the Cheddar Cliffs and Beachy Head," but these would be the exceptions, for

> thousands of square miles, which are now rich corn land and meadow, intersected by green hedge-rows, and dotted with villages and pleasant country seats, would appear as moors overgrown with furze, or fens abandoned to wild ducks. We should see straggling huts built of wood and covered with thatch where we now see manufacturing towns and sea-ports renowned to the farthest ends of the world. The capital itself would shrink to dimensions not much exceeding those of its present suburb on the south of the Thames.

Macaulay then zooms in to give us precise details: we learn, for example, that the "litter of a farmyard gathered under the windows" of the typical country gentleman of the era, and that "cabbages and gooseberry bushes grew close to his hall door."[9]

Adams is just as ambitious, devoting six chapters to what could almost be a satellite reconnaissance of the United States in the year 1800, and only then getting around to Jefferson's inauguration. Like Macaulay, he focuses on particularities, such as the fact that there was then no road between Baltimore and Washington, only tracks that "meandered through forests," with stagecoach drivers choosing whichever "seemed least dangerous." But he also zooms out, as when he makes the larger point that "five million Americans struggling with the untamed continent seemed hardly more competent to their task than the beavers and buffalo which had for countless generations made bridges and roads of their own."[10]

So here we have two eminently Victorian gentlemen who would hardly have known what to make of Virginia Woolf—although she would have known what to make of them—manipulating time and space with just as much ease and aplomb as her hero/heroine Orlando does, or as the most accomplished operator of a time machine in science fiction might do. And they only occasionally wrinkle their frock coats along the way.

II.

I expressed skepticism, in the first chapter, about the utility of time machines in historical research. I especially advised against graduate students relying on them, because of the limited perspective you tend to get from being plunked down in some particular part of the past, and the danger of not getting back in time for your orals.[11] If you consider historical research itself as a kind of time machine, though, you'll immediately notice that its capabilities go well beyond what such devices in science fiction normally accomplish. For as the examples of Macaulay and Adams illustrate, historians have the capacity for selectivity, simultaneity, and the shifting of scale: they can select from the cacophony of events what they think is really important; they can be in several times and places at once; and they can zoom in and out between macroscopic and microscopic levels of analysis. Let me develop each of these points in greater detail.

Selectivity. To be transported, in a conventional time machine, to a particular point in the past would be to have significances imposed on you. Assuming your instruments were working properly, you could choose the time and place you'd like to visit, but once there you'd have little control: events would quickly overwhelm you, and you'd just have to cope. We all know the plot from there: you'd spend the rest of the novel dodging voracious velociraptors, or fending off the Black Death, or trying to persuade the locals that you're not really a witch or a wizard and should therefore be spared the stake.

In the historian's method of time travel, though, you impose significances on the past, not the other way around. By remaining in the present as you explore the past, you retain the initiative: you can, like Macaulay and Adams, defend Whiggery or discredit Jefferson. You can focus on kings and their courtiers, or on warfare and statecraft, or on the great religious, intellectual, or ideological movements of the day. Or you can follow Fernand Braudel's example in *The Mediterranean and the Mediterranean World in the Age of Philip II* by bringing that monarch on stage only after some nine hundred pages in which you've discussed the geography, the weather, the crops, the animals, the economy, and the institutions—everything, it seems, but the great man himself, who was in his day at the center of things but in this history certainly is not.[12]

Who would have anticipated that we would today be studying the Inquisition through the eyes of a sixteenth-century Italian miller, or prerevolutionary France from the perspective of a recalcitrant Chinese manservant, or the first years of American independence from the experiences of a New England midwife? Works like Carlo Ginzburg's *The Cheese and the Worms*, Jonathan Spence's *The Question of Hu*, and Laurel Thatcher Ulrich's *A Midwife's Tale* result from the fortunate preservation of sources that open windows into another time.[13] But it's the historian here who *selects* what's significant, no less than would have been the case with a more traditional account of, say, the Battle of Hastings, or the life of Louis XIV. Millions of people over thousands of years have crossed the Rubicon, E. H. Carr pointed out in *What Is History?* We decide which ones we want to write about.[14]

It's an unsettling exercise to try to guess what historians two or three hundred years hence will select as significant about our age. One depressing possibility might be the defunct websites we leave lying around in cyberspace. For if Robert Darnton can reconstruct early eighteenth-century Parisian society on the basis of bookseller reports, gossip-filled scandal sheets, and accounts of the trial, torturing, and execution of aristocrats' cats, imagine what someone like him might do with what will remain of us.[15] All we can say for sure is that we'll only in part be remembered for what we consider significant about ourselves, or from what we choose to leave behind in the documents and the artifacts that will survive us. Future historians will have to choose what to make of these: it's they who will impose meanings, just as it's we who study the past, not those who lived through it, who do so.[16]

Simultaneity. Even more striking than selectivity is the capacity history gives you for simultaneity, for the ability to be *at once* in more than a single place or time. To achieve this, in science fiction, would no doubt require wormholes, beam splitters, and all kinds of other complicated devices; moreover, the plot, we can assume, would quickly lose its focus. Historians routinely frequent many places at once, though: their investigations of the past can extend to multiple subjects within the same period, as my examples from Macaulay and Adams illustrate, or to multiple points in time within the same subject, as traditional narratives do, or to some combination of both.

Consider John Keegan's classic accounts of Agincourt, Waterloo, and the Somme in *The Face of Battle.* No one could have witnessed those engagements in their entirety, nor could anyone have compared them on the basis of direct experience. And yet Keegan is able to take us there—in an Orlando-like extension of time horizons—to let us see all three battles with appalling clarity, even though as he himself acknowledges in the first line of the book: "I have not been in a battle; nor near one, nor heard one from afar, nor seen the aftermath."[17]

Or, for simultaneity in space at a particular time, there is Stephen Kern's remarkable but neglected book *The Culture of Time and Space,* which brings together developments in diplomacy, technology, and the arts in Europe and the United States on the eve of World War I to document an acceleration in the pace of events and a departure from traditional modes of representing them that could hardly have been visible while it was happening. Even Virginia Woolf waited until 1924 to make her famous observation that "on or about December, 1910, human character changed."[18]

It's only by standing apart from the events they describe, as Keegan and Kern do, that historians can understand and, more significantly, *compare* events. For surely understanding implies comparison:

to comprehend something is to see it in relation to other entities of the same class; but when these stretch over spans of time and space that exceed the physical capabilities of the individual observer, our only alternative is to be in several places at once.[19] Only viewing the past from the perspective of the present—the posture of Friedrich's wanderer on his mountaintop—allows you to do that.

Scale. A third way in which historians' time machines exceed the capability of those in science fiction is the ease with which they can shift the scale from the macroscopic to the microscopic, and back again. In one sense there's nothing surprising here, for this is the basis for a fundamental tool of narrative, the illustrative anecdote. Anytime a historian uses a particular episode to make a general point, scale shifting is taking place: the small, because it's easily described, is used to characterize the large, which may not be. In another sense, though, the results of this procedure can be startling.

A good example appears in the work of William H. McNeill, who, after completing his magisterial study *The Rise of the West* almost four decades ago, began producing a series of books that start from microscopic insights into human nature but then expand them into macroscopic reinterpretations of an extended past. The first of these focused quite literally on the microscopic: *Plagues and Peoples*, published in 1976, dealt with the effects of infectious diseases on world history. What McNeill showed was that great macro-events—the decline of Rome, the Mongol invasions, the European conquest of North and South America—can't be satisfactorily explained apart from the workings of micro-processes we've only come to understand in the last hundred years. What's known now about immunities or their absence projects a new angle of vision back into the past. This particular form of time travel only works, though, when the historian is prepared to shift scales: to consider how phenomena so small that they totally escaped notice at the time could shape phenomena so large that we've always wondered why they occurred.[20]

McNeill then did something similar in *The Pursuit of Power* (1982), where he focused on the role of new military technologies in determining the location and extent of political power over the past thousand years, and more recently in *Keeping Together in Time* (1995), which showed how so a simple matter as mass rhythmic movement—dance, drill, exercise—could provide a basis for social cohesiveness and hence for human organization.[21] What these books have in common is travel across not only time and space but also scale: the ability to select, to be in several places at once, to see processes at work that are visible to us now but were not then.

III.

Historians have no choice but to engage in these manipulations of time, space, and scale—these departures from literal representation—because a truly literal representation of any entity could only be the entity itself, and that would be impractical. David Hackett Fischer, whose list of historians' fallacies has delighted several generations of their students, provides a crisp explanation of why this is the case. The holist fallacy, he writes, "is the mistaken idea that a historian should select significant details from a sense of the whole thing." The problem with this approach is that "it would prevent a historian from knowing anything until he knows everything, which is absurd and impossible." The historian's evidence "is always incomplete, his perspective is always limited, and the thing itself is a vast expanding universe of particular events, about which an infinite number of facts or true statements can be discovered."[22]

What Fischer has described, one of my more mathematically inclined students has pointed out to me, is a problem in set theory. The easiest way to understand this is to take all whole numbers (1, 2, 3, 4, 5, and so on) and extract from the set all odd numbers (1, 3, 5, 7, 9, and so on): you wind up with just as many numbers as you started out with. The subset has as many units—an infinite number—as the whole set. The part is as great as the whole.[23] The physicist Stephen Hawking makes a similar point when he begins his *A Brief History of Time* with an anecdote about a lecturer explaining the workings of the solar system. At the end of the presentation, a little old lady in the back of the room gets up and announces firmly: "What you have told us is rubbish. The world is really a flat plate supported on the back of a giant tortoise." "What is the tortoise standing on?" the lecturer asks patiently. She replies: "It's tortoises all the way down."[24]

The answer isn't as flaky as you might think, because when it comes to the dimensions of time and space with which historians have to deal, it really is tortoises all the way down: time and space are infinitely divisible. We've agreed, as a matter of convenience, to measure time by a series of arbitrary units called centuries, decades, years, months, days, minutes, and seconds—historians don't normally go beyond these. But they could, for there are milliseconds, nanoseconds, and goodness knows what else at one end of the scale, just as there are light years, parsecs, and such at the other end of it.

To try to capture everything that happened to an ordinary person on an ordinary day in an ordinary place took James Joyce over seven hundred pages in *Ulysses*. So imagine turning Joyce loose on an account, say, of Napoleon at Waterloo. The level of detail would be such that most readers would nod off before the great man (Napoleon, I mean, not Joyce) had even got his underwear on. If indeed he wore underwear, a point I'm content to leave to whoever feels the need to divide history down to this level.[25]

This same principle of divisibility applies to space. Consider the meteorologist Lewis Richardson's famous question: how long is the coastline of Britain? The answer is that there is no answer—it depends. Are you measuring in miles, meters, or microns? The result will differ in each instance, and not just as a consequence of converting from one unit of measurement to another. For the further down you go in the scale of measurement, the more irregularities of coastline you'll pick up, so that the length will expand or contract in relation to the manner in which you're measuring it. And yet, as an object lodged in space, Britain is obviously a finite entity which does not inflate or deflate according to how we look at it. It's the modes with which we measure it that do.[26]

So once again, as with Napoleon, we make an estimate and move on. No one can know everything the emperor did on the disastrous day. No one can know, if Richardson is right, how far it actually is from London to Oxford. And yet people manage to find their way between these points all the time, some of them even reading about Napoleon at Waterloo as they do so.

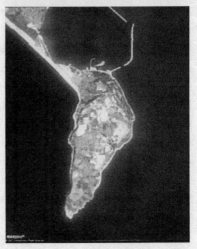

Three views of the British coastline. The Bill of Portland, barely visible in the first image, shows up as a small peninsula in the second and in detail in the third. Measurements based on each would produce different results for the coastline's length, and yet all three accurately represent the same coastline (GlobeXplorer).

If our methods of measurement render entities infinitely divisible into other entities, as set theory suggests they do, then the only defense against going bonkers in attempting to deal with this problem is to glide grandly over it, rather in the manner of Virginia Woolf. We have no choice but to sketch what we cannot precisely delineate, to generalize, to abstract. What this means, though, is that our modes of representation determine whatever it is we're representing. We're back with the historians' equivalent of the Heisenberg uncertainty principle: the act of observation alters what's being observed. Which means that objectivity as a consequence is hardly possible, and that there is, therefore, no such thing as truth. Which in turn means that postmodernism, which asserts all of these things, is confirmed.[27] Q.E.D. Or so it might seem.

IV.

But before we accept that unsettling conclusion, we should probe a little more deeply into the nature of time and space, as historians understand them. Leibniz defined time elegantly as "the order of non-contemporaneous things."[28] This isn't completely satisfactory, because words like "order" and "contemporaneous" all themselves depend on a conception of time, so that the word is defined in terms of itself. It's hard to see how we can do much better, though, for if truth be told we define ourselves in just the same way: to say what we are is to reflect what we've become. We cannot therefore stand apart from time: it is, as Marc Bloch wrote, "the very plasma in which events are immersed, and the field within which they become intelligible."[29]

How, then, do we think and write about something of which we're a part? We do it first, I believe, by noting that although time itself is a seamless continuum, it doesn't look that way to those who exist within it. Anyone with even a minimal level of consciousness would see time as divided, like ancient Gaul, into three parts: what lies in the past, what is yet to come in the future, and—most difficult of all to pin down—that elusive entity we know as the present.

St. Augustine doubted that the present even exists, describing it as something that "flies with such speed from future to past, as not to be lengthened out with the least stay."[30] But the historian R. G. Collingwood, writing some fifteen centuries later, took just the opposite view: "The present alone is actual," he insisted, using an Oxford illustration; the past and future had no existence comparable to the way in which, "when we are walking up the High past Queen's, Magdalen and All Souls exist."[31] So what's the problem here?

It may be that neither Augustine nor Collingwood had heard of singularities, those strange things that exist at the bottom of black holes (if black holes have bottoms) which cannot be measured, but which nonetheless transform all measurable objects that pass through them.[32] I prefer to think of the present as a singularity—or a funnel, if you prefer a more mundane metaphor, or a wormhole, if you favor a more exotic one—through which the future has got to pass in order to become the past. The present achieves this transformation by locking into place relationships between continuities and contingencies: on the future side of the singularity, these are fluid, decoupled, and therefore indeterminate; however, as they pass through it they fuse and cannot then be separated. The effect is that of DNA strands combining, or of a zipper that zips up but not back down.

By continuities, I mean patterns that extend across time. These are not laws, like gravity or entropy; they are not even theories, like relativity or natural selection. They are simply phenomena that recur with sufficient regularity to make themselves apparent to us. Without such patterns, we'd have no basis for generalizing about human experience: we'd not know, for example, that birth rates tend to decline as economic development advances, or that empires tend to expand beyond their means, or that democracies tend not to go to war with one another. But because these patterns show up so frequently in the past, we can reasonably expect them to continue to do so in the future. Trends that have held up over several hundred years are not apt to reverse themselves within the next several weeks.

By contingencies, I mean phenomena that do not form patterns.

These may include the actions individuals take for reasons known only to themselves: a Hitler on a grandiose scale, for example, or a Lee Harvey Oswald on a very particular one. They can involve what the chaos theorists call "sensitive dependence on initial conditions," situations where an imperceptible shift at the beginning of a process can produce enormous changes at the end of it.[33] They may result from the intersection of two or more continuities: students of accidents know that when predictable processes come together in unprecedented ways, unpredictable consequences can follow.[34] What all of these phenomena have in common is that they don't fall within the realm of repeated and therefore familiar experience: we generally learn about them only after they've happened.

We might define the future, then, as the zone within which contingencies and continuities coexist independently of one another; the past as the place where their relationship is inextricably fixed; and the present as the singularity that brings the two together, so that continuities intersect contingencies, contingencies encounter continuities, and through this process history is made.[35] And even though time itself isn't structured this way, for anyone who's stuck within time — and who isn't? — this distinction between past, present, and future is close to universal. We perceive time in a manner relevant to ourselves: as Woolf pointed out, though, there's a difference between what it actually is and the way in which we represent it.

V.

So much for time; what about space? For our purposes, let us define it simply as the location in which events occur, with the understanding that "events" are those passages from the future through the present into the past.[36] There is, at first glance, no comparably universal perception of space divided into distinct parts, as there is with time. The familiar dimensions of height, width, and depth are conventions we rely upon to measure space, much as we use hours, minutes, and seconds to measure time. They aren't *conceptions* of space, though, analogous to our divisions of time into past, present, and future.

If there is such a division for space, I suspect it lies in the distinction between the actual and the cartographic. The making of maps must be as ancient and ubiquitous a practice as is our three-part conception of time. Both reduce the infinitely complex to a finite, manageable, frame of reference.[37] Both involve the imposition of artificial grids—hours and days, longitude and latitude—on temporal and spatial landscapes, or perhaps I should say on timescapes and landscapes. Both provide a way of reversing divisibility, of retrieving unity, of recapturing a *sense* of the whole, even though it can never *be* the whole.

For to try to represent everything that's in a particular landscape would be as absurd as to attempt to recount everything that actually happened, whether at Waterloo or anywhere else. Such a map, like such an account, would have to *become* what it represented, a circumstance imagined only by such connoisseurs of the ridiculous as Lewis Carroll or Jorge Luis Borges. Borges writes, for example, of an empire in which:

> the Art of Cartography attained such Perfection that . . . . the Cartographers Guilds struck a map of the Empire whose size was that of the Empire, and which coincided point for point with it. The following Generations, who were not so fond of the Study of Cartography . . . , saw that that vast Map was Useless, and . . . they delivered it up to the Inclemencies of Sun and Winters. In the Deserts of the West, still today, there are Tattered Ruins of that Map, inhabited by Animals and Beggars.[38]

We avoid the literal in making maps because to do otherwise would not be to *represent* at all but rather to *replicate*. We'd find ourselves drowning in detail: the *distillation* that's required for the comprehension and transmission of vicarious experience would be lost.

Maps do exactly that: they distill the experiences of others for the purpose of helping you get from where you are to where you want to go. Think how much time we'd waste if everyone going from Oxford to London had to find their own way, like molecules bouncing around in a beaker or monkeys poised before computer keyboards. Think how risky it would be to send ships to sea without any means of knowing the locations of rocks and shoals. Think how perilous air travel would become without the radios, radar, and now satellite guidance systems that create virtual pathways through a featureless sky. Whether they take the form of crude markings in the sand or of the most sophisticated computer graphics, maps have in common, as do the works of historians, a *packaging of vicarious experience*.

But despite their obvious utility, there's no such thing as a single correct map.[39] The form of the map reflects its purpose. A highway map will exaggerate certain features of the landscape and neglect others: you need to be able to see the routes, their numbers, and the cities they run between. You don't need to know the nature of the soil, or the vegetation, or (except maybe in certain parts of California) the geologic fault lines to be found along the way. Much the same is true of scale: you'd not plot an automobile trip on a globe, but you might very well an intercontinental airplane route. No map tells you everything it's possible to know. They do generally tell you enough, though, to get you from here to there, and that's generally sufficient.

VI.

So what if we were to think of history as a kind of mapping? If, as I suggested earlier, the past is a landscape and history is the way we represent it, then this might make sense. It would establish the linkage between pattern recognition as the primary form of human perception and the fact that all history—even the most simple narrative—draws upon the recognition of such patterns. It would permit varying levels of detail, not just as a reflection of scale but also of the information available at any given time about a particular landscape, geographical or historical. But, most important, this metaphor would allow us to get closer to the way historians know when they've got it right.

For verification in cartography takes place by *fitting* representations to reality. You have the physical landscape, but you wouldn't want to try to replicate it. You have, in your mind, reasons for representing the landscape: you want to find your way through it without having to rely on your own immediate senses; hence you draw on the generalized experience of others. And you have the map itself, which results from fitting together what is actually there with what the user of the map needs to know about what is there.

The fit becomes more precise the more the landscape is investigated. The first maps of newly discovered territories are usually crude sketches of a coastline, with lots of blank spaces and perhaps a few sea monsters or dragons occupying them. As exploration proceeds, the map's features become more specific and the beasts tend to disappear. In time, there'll be multiple maps of the same territory prepared for different purposes, whether to show roads, towns, rivers, mountains, resources, topography, geology, population, weather, or even the volume of traffic—and hence the probability of traffic jams—along the routes marked out on other maps.

Cartographic verification is, therefore, entirely relative: it depends upon how well the mapmaker achieves a *fit* between the landscape that's being mapped and the requirements of those for whom the map is being made. And yet, despite this indeterminacy, I know of no postmodernist who would deny the existence of landscapes, or that it's useful to represent them. It would be most unwise for sailors to conclude, simply because we cannot specify the length of the British coastline, that it isn't there and that they can sail self-confidently through it. So too it would be imprudent for historians to decide, from the fact that we have no absolute basis for measuring time and space, that they can't know anything about what happened within them.

Chapter Three

STRUCTURE AND PROCESS

HISTORICAL LANDSCAPES DIFFER from cartographic landscapes, however, in one important respect: they are physically inaccessible to us. Anyone mapping even the most remote regions of the earth's surface can visit or at least photograph the terrain in question. Historians can't do that. "No Egyptologist has ever seen Ramses," Marc Bloch points out in *The Historian's Craft.* "No expert on the Napoleonic Wars has ever heard the sound of the cannon at Austerlitz." Historians "are in the predicament of a police magistrate who strives to reconstruct a crime he has not seen; of a physicist who, confined to his bed with the grippe, hears the results of his experiments only through the reports of his laboratory technician." As a consequence, the historian "never arrives until after the experiment has been concluded. But, under favorable circumstances, the experiment leaves behind certain residues which he can see with his own eyes."[1]

If time and space provide the *field* in which history happens, then, structure and process provide the *mechanism.* For it is from structures that survive into the present—the "certain residues" of which Bloch wrote—that we reconstruct processes inaccessible to us because they took place in the past. "A historical fact is an inference from the relics," the sociologist John Goldthorpe has observed.[2] These may include bones and excrement, tools and weapons, great ideas and works of art, or documents that get deposited in archives; but in each case processes produced them. We can know these only from the structures they leave behind.

A good way to visualize this is to consider the humble roadcut. Geologists love them because they expose tilts, folds, and uncomformities in strata, structures from which one can derive processes extending back millions and even billions of years. They are, as John McPhee has put it, "windows into the world as it was in other times."[3] Roadcuts wouldn't exist, though, were it not for decisions made, so recently as to remain within the geologic present, to construct the canals, railways, and highways that required them.[4] For geologists, then, the distinction between structure and process corresponds to

The Sideling Hill roadcut, I-68, in western Maryland
(courtesy of the Maryland Geological Survey; photo by Paul Breeding).

the one between the present, where structures exist, and the past, where processes produced them. Does it also for historians? That's the question I want to explore here, and the best place to start is with the old debate over whether history is, or isn't, a science.

I.

"When I was very young," E. H. Carr commented in his 1961 Trevelyan lectures at Cambridge, "I was suitably impressed to learn that, appearances notwithstanding, the whale is not a fish. Nowadays these questions of classification move me less; and it does not worry me unduly when I am assured that history is not a science."[5] If you were to deconstruct that statement, you could give it several possible meanings. One is that history is indeed a science. The second is that it isn't. The third is that Carr had the habit of sweeping away ambiguities, rather in the way that Oxford and Cambridge college waiters, at high table, sweep away crumbs.[6]

I'm inclined to think, though—and Carr's own lectures suggest this—that the question can't be dismissed quite so easily. For science has one quality that privileges it above all other modes of inquiry: it has shown itself more capable than any of the others at eliciting agreement on the validity of results across cultures, in different languages, and among highly dissimilar observers. The structure of the DNA molecule looks much the same to researchers in Switzerland, Singapore, and Sri Lanka. Aircraft wings bear stress similarly whether the airlines that rely on them operate as subsidized state monopolies or adventurous entrepreneurial enterprises. Astronomers of Christian, Muslim, and Buddhist persuasions have little difficulty reaching a consensus on what causes eclipses, or how galaxies move.

There are of course other ways to resolve issues like these. You could, for example, probe the entrails of animals, read tea leaves, consult a horoscope, seek divine guidance, or make inquiries in an Internet chat room. You'd certainly get results, but you'd not get very many other people to agree on the accuracy of the results. The advantage of science, John Ziman has pointed out, is that it provides "a consensus of rational opinion over the widest possible field."[7]

To be sure, we can't expect the methods of science to work with equal precision, or to command comparably broad assent, when it comes to the study of human affairs. The reason is obvious: consciousness—perhaps I should say willfulness—can override the kinds of laws that govern the behavior of molecules, or air flows, or celestial objects. People, the political scientist Stanley Hoffmann once reminded his colleagues, are not "gases or pistons."[8] I see no reason, however, why this difficulty should invalidate Ziman's standard as one historians ought to *try* to reach—a consensus of rational opinion over the widest possible field—even if they never actually get there.

You don't have to read very far in Carr to discover that, despite his pronouncement on whales and fishes, he thought so too. So did Marc Bloch. They both saw science as a model for historians, but not because they thought historians were becoming, or ought to become, more scientific. It was rather because *they saw scientists as becoming more historical*. With the nineteenth-century achievements of Charles Lyell in geology and Charles Darwin in biology, Carr noted, "[s]cience was concerned no longer with something static and timeless, but with a process of change and development."[9] Bloch argued similarly, focusing on twentieth-century developments:

> The kinetic theory of gases, Einstein's mechanics, and the quantum theory have profoundly altered that concept of science which, only yesterday, was unanimously accepted. . . . For certainty, they have often substituted the infinitely probable; for the strictly measurable, the notion of the eternal relativity of measurement. . . . Hence, we are much better prepared to admit that a scholarly discipline may pretend to the dignity of a science without insisting upon Euclidian demonstrations or immutable laws of repetition. . . . We no longer

feel obliged to impose upon every subject of knowledge a uniform intellectual pattern, borrowed from natural science, since even there, that pattern has ceased to be entirely applicable.[10]

By discovering that what exists in the present has not always done so in the past, that objects and organisms evolve through time instead of remaining the same for all time, scientists had begun to *derive structures from processes*: they had, in short, brought history into science. As a consequence of this shift from a static to an evolutionary view, Carr concluded, "the historian has some excuse for feeling himself more at home in the world of science today than he could have done a hundred years ago."[11]

Carr wrote those words four decades ago. Do they still make sense today? I think they do, provided you specify the *kind* of science you have in mind.

II.

The key to consensus, in science, is reproducibility: observations made under equivalent conditions, no matter who makes them, are expected to produce closely corresponding results.[12] Mathematicians recalculate *pi* to billions of decimal places with absolute confidence that its value will remain what it has been for thousands of years.[13] Physics and chemistry are only slightly less reliable, for although investigators can't always be sure of what's happening at subatomic levels, they do tend to get similar results when they perform laboratory experiments under similar conditions, and they probably always will. Verification, within these disciplines, takes place by repeating actual processes. Time and space are compressed and manipulated; history itself is in effect rerun. In that sense, obviously, the historical method can never approximate the scientific method.

But not all sciences work this way. In fields like astronomy, geology, paleontology, or evolutionary biology, phenomena rarely fit within laboratories, and the time required to see results can exceed the life spans of those who seek them.[14] These disciplines instead depend upon thought experiments: practitioners rerun in their minds—or perhaps now in their computer simulations—what their test tubes, centrifuges, and electron microscopes can't manage. They then look for evidence suggesting which of these mental exercises comes closest to explaining their physical observations. Reproducibility means building a consensus that such correspondences seem plausible. The only way these scientists can rerun history is to imagine it, but they must do so within the limits of logic. They can't attribute the inexplicable to pixies, wizards, or extraterrestrial visitors and still expect to persuade their peers that their findings are valid.[15]

How, apart from such thought experiments, could geologists account for the fact that strata that can only have been laid down horizontally nevertheless often wind up tilted, or even vertical? Or for granite that intrudes itself into limestone? Or for seashells that show up thousands of feet above, and hundreds of miles away from, the nearest sea?[16] How else could biologists make sense of organs with no apparent function: the whale's vestigial legs, for example, or the panda's thumb, or the human tail bone?[17] Why do human genes differ so little from those of fleas, worms, flies, monkeys, and mice?[18] How, for that matter, can astrophysicists explain the origins of the universe? In each of these instances, structures have survived that only past processes can explain: the geological uplift and collapse driven by plate tectonics, for example, or the evolution of species that results from natural selection, or the residual radiation left over from the Big Bang.

Laboratory experiments would hardly suffice to test such explanations. Darwin's required a time scale extending over hundreds of millions of years. Alfred Wegener visualized an entire earth on which continents could come together and drift apart. Albert Einstein's imagined experiments exceeded the size not just of his laboratory but of his galaxy. All of these scientific revolutionaries coupled imagination with logic to derive past processes from present structures. Nor were they in any way exceptional in this, for the same thing happens every day in natural history museums before critical audiences of small children. What's the reconstruction of dinosaurs and other ancient creatures from fossils, after all, if not a fitting of imagined flesh to surviving bones, or at least to impressions of them?[19] And the kids are, most of the time at least, suitably impressed.

It's here that the methods of historians and scientists—at least those scientists for whom reproducibility cannot take place in the laboratory—roughly coincide. For historians too start with surviving structures, whether they be archives, artifacts, or even memories. They then deduce the processes that produced them. Like geologists and paleontologists, they must allow for the fact that most sources from the past don't survive, and that most daily events don't even generate a survivable record in the first place. Like biologists and astrophysicists, they must deal with ambiguous or even contradictory evidence. And like all scientists who work outside of laboratories, historians must use logic and imagination to overcome the resulting difficulties, their own equivalent of thought experiments, if you will.

It's in this sense, I think, that R. G. Collingwood was correct when he insisted on the inseparability of the past from the historian's present: the present is where the thought experiments take place.[20] This doesn't mean, though, that the past didn't exist, for without it there'd be nothing to experiment upon. To illustrate this point, let me cite two very different examples of how historians use the laboratory that's in their mind to reconstruct past processes from surviving structures.

Laurel Thatcher Ulrich's *A Midwife's Tale* recounts the life of Martha Ballard, a woman hardly anyone beyond her late eighteenth-century Maine village could have known about at the time, on the basis of a single surviving source: the laconic diary she kept, not for posterity, but for the purpose of recording payments for services rendered. Ulrich fleshes out this archival fossil—neglected by several generations of male historians—in several ways: by drawing on what's known from other sources about the time and place in which Ballard lived; by imagining how Ballard herself must have understood and sought to manage her situation; and by using contemporary gender and family relationships to compare it with what women experience today. The book is an exercise in historical paleontology, and it succeeds brilliantly.[21]

Jared Diamond's *Guns, Germs, and Steel*, conversely, works from a contemporary circumstance—the persistence of inequality throughout the world—to try to determine how it came about. He examines several cultures, some advanced, some not, that have survived into the present. He traces them back to their prehistoric roots when all societies were roughly equal, and then employs thought experiments to explain what happened to them along the way. His conclusions are striking: an east-west axis, as in Eurasia, allowed movement along more or less the same latitude and hence facilitated the interchange of people, economies, ideas, and—not least in importance—the germs that could build up immunities. A north-south axis, as in Africa and North and South America, impeded such movement. As a result in large part of plate tectonics, the Eurasians came to rule the world.[22]

It would be difficult to think of two more dissimilar works of history in terms of their scope and scale. And yet, in method they're much the same: each starts with a surviving structure—Ballard's diary in Ulrich's case, global inequality in Diamond's; each seeks, through thought experiments, to derive the processes that gave rise to that structure; each does so with an eye to the contemporary significance of those findings. They each combine logic with imagination. And they both won the Pulitzer Prize.

But don't novelists, poets, and playwrights also combine logic with imagination? They do, of course, although in a different way. Artists can, if they wish, conjure up their subjects out of thin air. Historians can't do this: their subjects must really have existed. Artists can coexist in time with their subjects, altering them as they please. Historians can never do this: they can alter their representations of a subject, but not the subject itself. The historian's imagination must be "sufficiently powerful to make his narrative affecting," Macaulay once wrote. "Yet he must control it so absolutely as to content himself with the materials which he finds, and to refrain from supplying deficiencies by additions of his own."[23] Imagination in history then, as in science, must be tethered to and disciplined by sources: that's what distinguishes it from the arts and all other methods of representing reality.

So is history a science? I put the question to a group of Yale seniors recently, and the answer one of them came up with made perfect sense to me: it was that we should instead concentrate on determining which sciences are historical.[24] The distinction would lie along the line separating *actual replicability* as the standard for verification—the rerunning of experiments in a laboratory—from the *virtual replicability* that's associated with thought experiments. And it would be the accessibility versus the inaccessibility of processes that would make the difference.

III.

No geologist has ever penetrated the surface of the earth beyond a few miles, and yet they self-confidently tell us how what happens down there causes continents to drift and earthquakes to occur up here. No paleontologist has ever actually seen a dinosaur, and yet they reconstruct the lives and deaths of these creatures in ways that convince their colleagues—to say nothing of small children—that they know what they're talking about. No astronomer has ever been beyond the earth's orbit, and yet from this very limited vantage point they map the universe. With the exception of a few biologists who've tracked the changing shapes of finches' beaks in the Galapagos, no one has ever witnessed the process of natural selection beyond the microscopic level, and yet an entire discipline is based on it.[25] And if all of this sounds like Marc Bloch on the absence of living witnesses to the Battle of Austerlitz, there's a good reason for that.

It is that both history and the evolutionary sciences practice the remote sensing of phenomena with which they can never directly interact. They are, metaphorically, in the position of Friedrich's wanderer on his mountaintop. They can't simply view the fog and mist, though: they must find ways to determine what lies beneath it, and to represent whatever they find in such a way as to persuade those for whom the representation is intended that it's reasonably accurate. Logic and imagination can certainly help; but there's also, I think, a particular *sequence of procedures* to be followed in accomplishing this task. Two quite different examples of remote sensing, one drawn from recent history, the other from prehistory, suggest what it is.

The first is arguably the most famous historical case of remote sensing, the discovery of Soviet medium- and intermediate-range missiles in Cuba in October 1962. The story begins with the discovery, by means of U-2 spy plane photoreconnaissance, of the missiles themselves, which Soviet leader Nikita Khrushchev and his advisers apparently thought could be deployed secretly on the island because they'd be indistinguishable from its palm trees.[26] This was an unexpected development, because hardly anyone in Washington had anticipated that the Kremlin leadership would behave in such a risky manner, or that its intelligence estimates—not least about the nature of palm trees—would be so bad. Other less provocative forms of military assistance had been expected, though, which is why the U-2s were flying over Cuba in the first place. When one of them detected structures resembling missile sites in the Soviet Union—known from earlier U-2 flights over that country—the photo-analysts realized instantly what they were seeing, even though they'd not been looking for it. By citing this comparison, they convinced President Kennedy that their conclusions made sense, a judgment then confirmed by subsequent U-2 missions.[27] You can break this episode down, therefore, into three stages: the reality on the ground, what the experts made of that reality, and what they could persuade their superiors to accept.

My second case comes from paleontologists, who also practice a

kind of remote sensing based on the analysis of bones, shells, and fossils. Representing the creatures that left these behind requires linking
precise observation and description of what's survived with the ability
to imagine what life must have been like hundreds of millions of years
ago. As in the Cuban missile crisis, newly discovered evidence has to
be compared with what's already known. More is involved than just
taxonomy, though, for paleontologists must also persuade their colleagues that their conclusions are plausible. They can't simply *assert*
that the allosaurus nurtured its young, or that the archaeopteryx is the
ancestor of today's birds; they must also *convince*. This too requires
fitting together three things: what remains from original sources; what
the paleontologists themselves make of what remains; and what they
can bring their fellow professionals to accept.[28]

In both of these cases, the discovery of structures led to the derivation of processes. The Cuba photographs forced Washington officials into a desperate scramble to try to determine why Khrushchev
had placed the missiles there—an important thing to know before
deciding on what should be done to get them out. Fossils suggesting
dinosaur nests and even feathers have forced paleontologists to reconsider what they thought they knew about where birds may have come
from. I don't want to push this comparison too far: it's a stretch, of
course, to link such dissimilar examples of remote sensing. It's precisely their dissimilarities in all other respects, though, that cause me
to think their procedural similarities significant.

Now return, if you will, to my cartographic metaphor from the previous chapter. Mapmakers also go through a three-stage process of
connecting reality, representation, and persuasion. They represent
realities they can't replicate and wouldn't want to: a truly accurate
map of Oxford would be an exact clone of Oxford and wouldn't easily
fit within backpacks or briefcases. Maps vary scale and content
according to need. A world map has a different purpose from one
intended to identify bicycle paths or garbage dumps. Nor are maps
free from preconceptions. There's always some prior reason for what's

shown, and not shown.[29] We evaluate maps according to their useful-ness: is the layout legible? Is the representation credible? Does the map extend our perceptions beyond what we ourselves can manage, so that it performs the practical task of getting us from here to there? As with the reconstruction of dinosaurs and the construction of history, there is again the reality to be represented, the representation itself, and its reception by those who use it.

"To construct a good . . . map," Jane Azevedo, one of the most interesting theorists of map-making, has pointed out,

> requires more than just a set of data and a simple truth-preserving mechanism by which to represent it. Given the purposes for which the map is to be used, there must be a theory of what relationships an appropriate map for that purpose is required to represent, to what degree of accuracy, and in what form. Where there are multiple interests, judgments must be made as to which is of prior importance, as they may not all be able to be represented with equal accuracy.

This relationship between data, modes of representation, and interests to be served in presenting the representation is not, however, a hierarchical one: it's rather, as she demonstrates, "a reiteration loop."

> The map is a function of both the data and the theory. The data selected is a function of the theory. Both the map and the theory may have to be modified in the light of the data. Finally, the map may itself bring about change in the theory. All levels of the hierarchy are subject to modification in interaction with the other levels.[30]

I like this notion of a "reiteration loop" because it privileges neither inductive or deductive modes of inquiry.[31] The remote sensing of processes by way of surviving structures—whether in history or science—functions similarly. For to begin with such a structure, as all his-

torians and evolutionary scientists must, is a deductive act: the task is
to deduce the processes that produced it. You can hardly perform that
task, though, without repeated acts of induction: you have to survey
the evidence, sense what's there, and find ways to represent it. Finding
those ways, though, gets you back to the deductive level, for you must
deduce them from the interests of those for whom the representation
is being made. It makes little sense, then, to try to align structure and
process neatly with deduction and induction. What's required instead
is to apply both techniques to the objects of your inquiry, fitting each to
the other as seems most appropriate to the task at hand.[32]

An easier way to think about this is to imagine yourself as a tailor.
Clothes make it possible for people to appear in public: tailors are the
intermediaries between society and naked bodies.[33] But unless you
were working for, say, Mao Zedong, you wouldn't want to dress all your
customers in exactly the same way. You'd want to allow for their varying shapes and sizes. You'd probably want to reflect their preferences
as to fabric, style, and ornamentation. You would, in this sense, be *representing* them to a world in which they wouldn't want to be seen as
they really are. But since you'd have a professional reputation to
uphold, you'd also be representing yourself: you wouldn't want to deck
your clients out, these days, in bell-bottom trousers or polyester
leisure suits. You might even want to try to shift current fashions a bit
by coming up with a style others might emulate. Once again, though,
the "fit" would have to extend across three levels: the body to be
clothed, the design of the clothing, and the world of fashion that
would either embrace, reject, or ignore what results.

I find these metaphors useful in explaining how historians work,
for like paleontologists, cartographers, and tailors we seek a good "fit"
across three distinct levels of activity. In recounting an event, or a
series of them, we begin with what's there—normally archives, the
equivalent for us of bones, bodies, or terrain. We interpret these
through our own distinctive viewpoints: it's here that imagination,
even dramatization, is involved. Ultimately, though, the product must

go before an audience, at which point one of several things may happen. The patrons may approve because what they see confirms their preconceptions. They may disapprove if it does not. Or—and this is what paleontologists, tailors, and cartographers as well as historians hope for—the product may move those who encounter it to revise their own views so that a new basis for critical judgment emerges, perhaps even a new view of reality itself.

IV.

Some years ago I asked the great global historian William H. McNeill to explain his method of writing history to a group of social, physical, and biological scientists attending a conference I'd organized. He at first resisted doing this, claiming that he had no particular method. When pressed, though, he described it as follows:

> I get curious about a problem and start reading up on it. What I read causes me to redefine the problem. Redefining the problem causes me to shift the direction of what I'm reading. That in turn further reshapes the problem, which further redirects the reading. I go back and forth like this until it feels right, then I write it up and ship it off to the publisher.

McNeill's presentation elicited expressions of disappointment, even derision, from the economists, sociologists, and political scientists present. "That's not a method," several of them exclaimed. "It's not parsimonious, it doesn't distinguish between independent and dependent variables, it hopelessly confuses induction and deduction." But then there came a deep voice from the back of the room. "Yes, it is," it growled. "That's exactly how we do physics!"[34]

"[T]he validation of a theoretical model by appeal to experiment is not a mechanical process," John Ziman has written. "It hinges on the expert judgements of physicists, who must decide for themselves whether there is an *adequate fit* between theory and experiment, given the uncertainties of the data and the unavoidable idealizations of the mathematical analysis. The skill to make such judgements comes from experience."[35] But if that's right—if science really privileges neither induction nor deduction, if it relies to such an extent on intuition and judgment, if in the final analysis its findings can't be separated from the characteristics of those who do the finding—then our stereotypical view of the scientific method, which denies all of those things, will need revision. "Scientists . . . do not think in straight lines," Edward O. Wilson has pointed out. "They contrive concepts, evidence, relevance, connections, and analysis as they go along, parsing it all into fragments and in no particular order. . . . Perhaps only openly confessional memoirs, still rare to nonexistent, might disclose how scientists actually find their way to a publishable conclusion."[36] In short, they think like—William H. McNeill.

That news may upset some social scientists, but let us leave that problem for the next chapter. What I'd like to focus on here is the particular procedure that seems common to both historical and scientific reasoning as McNeill, Ziman, and Wilson understand it: it's our own earlier notion, derived from cartography, of *fitting things together*.

There's an old name for this that's coming back into fashion: *consilience*. It originated with the nineteenth-century Cambridge philosopher of science William Whewell, who used it to describe "unexpected coincidences of results drawn from distant parts of [a] subject."[37] Wilson has recently revived the term as a way of asking "whether, in the gathering of disciplines, specialists can ever reach agreement on a common body of abstract principles and evidentiary proof." It's significant, I think, that he places history at the center of these disciplines, pointing out that it's "not enough to say that human action is historical, and that history is an unfolding of unique events." For:

> Nothing fundamental separates the course of human history from the course of physical history, whether in the stars or in organic diversity. Astronomy, geology, and evolutionary biology are examples

of primarily historical disciplines linked by consilience to the rest of the natural sciences. . . . [I]f ten thousand humanoid histories could be traced on ten thousand Earthlike planets, and from a comparative study of those histories empirical tests and principles evolved, [then] historiography—the explanation of historical trends—would already be a natural science.[38]

Unfortunately, that's about as far as Wilson goes in developing the connection, by way of consilience, between the historical sciences on the one hand and the natural sciences on the other. I wonder, though, whether Whewell's concept of "unexpected coincidences," or perhaps more usefully "fitting together," might not give us a point of departure for further investigation.

It would largely reside in the power of metaphor. Most of what I've said so far has been based on the premise that the doing of history is "like" certain other things: I've made analogies to painting, cartography, and even tailoring as well as to mathematics, astronomy, geology, paleontology, and evolutionary biology. I've done so without the slightest sense that history can or should *imitate* these disciplines: certainly Wilson's vision of ten thousand humanoid histories is a long way off. I do think, though, that by *comparing* what they do to what happens in other fields, historians might accomplish several useful things:

First, they might better justify their own existence. Historians ought to be as adept as the practitioners of other disciplines are at defending their methods—but they aren't. Bloch noted the problem with eerie prescience as early as 1942:

Surely, in a world which stands upon the threshold of the chemistry of the atom, which is only beginning to fathom the mystery of interstellar space, in this poor world of ours which, however justifiably proud of its science, has created so little happiness for itself, the tedious minutiae of historical erudition, easily capable of consuming a whole lifetime, would deserve condemnation as an absurd waste of energy, bordering on the criminal, were they to end merely by coating one of our diversions with a thin veneer of truth. Either all minds capable of better employment must be dissuaded from the practice of history, or history must prove its legitimacy as a form of knowledge.[39]

Carr put it more bluntly in 1961: "those historians who today pretend to dispense with a philosophy of history are merely trying, vainly and self-consciously, like members of a nudist colony, to recreate the Garden of Eden in their garden suburb."[40] Methodological innocence leads to methodological vulnerability. Comparisons could give historians the means of covering themselves.

Second, comparisons could clarify the ways in which other disciplines relate to our own. Similarities in subject don't necessarily ensure similarities in method, a point Bloch and Carr were trying to make by stressing the compatibility of historians' methods with those of the natural scientists. The implication was that the social sciences, in which static models are still valued and evolution is often regarded as a messy nuisance, might not be the place historians should look for the analogies that might help them define themselves.

Finally, such comparisons might bolster our own self-confidence. Historians too often retreat in confusion when social scientists reproach them for not using equations, graphs, matrices, and the other methods of formal modeling to represent the past. We're not being "scientific," we're told, when we subvert generalizations, resist ranking causes, and reject the use of discipline-specific jargon. We might well respond, though, by asking: what are zoologists and botanists doing when they seek out distinctive species? Or: how would an astronomer rank the causes that produced the solar system, or the earth's position within it? Or: why do so many "hard" scientists write so much better than most social scientists—and have so many more readers?[41] Such responses might not satisfy our critics. But they would certainly boost our morale.

I'll focus, in the next chapter, on what separates historical from social scientific thinking: on the paradox that, despite the similarities in our subject matter, there are such differences in the way in which historians and social scientists think about it. These largely revolve around the question of whether there can ever be such a thing as a truly independent variable.

Chapter Four

THE INTERDEPENDENCY OF VARIABLES

NOT LONG AGO I attended a conference at a distinguished American university with an equally distinguished group of political scientists. The subject was case studies—how to do them, and in particular how to extract meaningful generalizations from them. During the presentations, there was a good deal of talk, as there always seems to be when social scientists gather, about the need to distinguish independent from dependent variables. The single most frequently asked question was: "How can we tease out the independent variable?"

I'd participated in many such meetings in the past and had always found it hard to answer such queries. This was partly because all this talk about "teasing out" had me imagining my scholarly colleagues as hairdressers, which was distracting. The larger problem, though, was that historians don't think in terms of independent and dependent variables. We assume the interdependency of variables as we trace their interconnections through time. Sorting them into separate categories just isn't very useful to us.

For some reason on this occasion, though, I innocently raised my hand and inquired: "How, apart from God if he or she exists, can there ever be such a thing as an independent variable? Aren't all variables dependent on other variables?" Naturally I'd expected a quick and clear answer to so simple a question. But to my great surprise, there was a brief period of silence around the table during which an exchange of what I can only call blank looks took place. Whereupon our chair said: "Well, moving right along . . ."

My first inclination was not to make too much of this. Perhaps my question had been *so* naïve that the silence was a polite way of expressing astonishment that anyone would ask it. The more I pondered the matter, though, the more I realized that I'd inadvertently exposed an assumption sufficiently basic that practitioners of a discipline take it for granted, and hence find it difficult to explain or to justify.[1] Still further reflection raised the possibility that this specific difference in how historians and political scientists operate might reflect a larger divergence in methods of inquiry that separates history from the social sciences generally.

It is, most fundamentally, the distinction between a *reductionist* and an *ecological* view of reality. I'd like to explore that difference in this chapter, focusing especially on how it might relate to the distinction between laboratory and non-laboratory sciences that I discussed in the previous one—between those sciences that can rerun experiments and those that can't. I'll then want to consider what this might suggest about the gap between historical and social scientific thinking that my naïve question about independent variables so unexpectedly revealed.

I.

I take reductionism to be the belief that you can best understand reality by breaking it up into its various parts. In mathematical terms, you seek the variable within an equation that determines the value of all the others. Or, more broadly, you search for the element whose removal from a causal chain would alter the outcome. It's critical to reductionism that causes be ranked hierarchically. To invoke a democracy of causes—to suggest that an event may have had many antecedents—is considered to be, well, mushy.[2] As an influential recent guide to social science method puts it:

> A successful project is one that explains a lot with a little. At best, the goal is to use a single explanatory variable to explain numerous observations on dependent variables. A research design that explains a lot with a lot is not very informative. . . .[3]

Reductionism implies, therefore, that there are indeed independent variables, and that we can know what they are.

But when you're accounting for the evolution of life forms, or the drifting of continents, or the formation of galaxies, you can hardly break things up into their component parts, because so much depends upon so much else. Species survive, or become extinct, not by virtue of some innate superiority or deficiency, but because of the success with which they adapt to the environment that surrounds them. Fault lines are difficult to explain without an understanding of tectonic plates and the interconnected processes that move them around on the surface of the earth. Gravity ensures that the shape and location of a particular galaxy will be affected, even if only slightly, by the existence of all the other galaxies. Sciences like astronomy, geology, and paleontology operate, in short, from an ecological view of reality.[4]

Reductionism, then, is hardly the only mode of scientific investigation. For while the ecological approach also values the specification of simple components, it does not stop with that: it considers how components interact to become systems whose nature can't be defined merely by calculating the sum of their parts. It allows for fundamental particles, but it seeks to place them within an equally fundamental universe. The ecological viewpoint is inclusive, even as the reductionist perspective is exclusive; but would anyone claim that inclusion is any less "scientific" a procedure than exclusion? Or that sciences that rely upon one of these methods are somehow superior to those that use the other?[5]

It's worth asking, therefore, where the pressure for reductionism within the social sciences actually comes from. The answer, I think, is that these disciplines prefer reductionist over ecological methods of inquiry because they see in reductionism the only feasible way to generalize about the past in such a way as to be able to forecast the future.[6]

II.

The trouble with the future is that it's so much less knowable than the past. Because it lies on the other side of the singularity that is the present, all we can count on is that certain continuities from the past will extend into it, and that they will there encounter uncertain contingencies. Some continuities will be sufficiently robust that contingencies will not deflect them: time will continue to pass; gravity will keep us from flying off into space; people will still be born, grow old, and die. When it comes to actions people themselves choose to take, though—when consciousness itself becomes a contingency—forecasting becomes a far more problematic enterprise.

The social sciences have too often dealt with this problem by denying its existence. They've operated from the conviction that consciousness and the behavior that results from it are subject, at least in general terms, to the workings of rules—if not laws—whose existence we can detect and whose effects we can describe. Once we've done this, or so many social scientists over many years have assumed, we'll then be able to accomplish in the realm of human affairs at least some of the tasks of explanation and forecasting that the natural sciences routinely perform.[7]

There are multiple examples of this approach—I'll mention only six of them here: (1) "rational choice" assumptions in economics and political science, which maintain that people calculate their own best interests objectively and on the basis of accurate information about the circumstances within which these exist; (2) "structural functionalism" in sociology, which sees institutions as necessary components of the particular social structures within which they are embedded; (3) "modernization" theory, which insists that all nations go through similar stages of economic development; (4) the "where you stand depends on where you sit" argument in organizational studies—also known as Miles's Law—which explains the behavior of bureaucracies, large and small, in terms of an overriding concern with self-perpetuation; (5) Freudian psychology, which seeks to account for the actions of individuals by invoking a set of unconscious impulses and inhibitions inherited—by everyone—from childhood; and (6) "realist" and "neorealist" theories of international relations, which claim that all nations seek, in all situations, to maximize their power.

Now these are, to be sure, gross oversimplifications, certain to elicit howls of protest from practitioners in these fields. I think they may stand, though, as reflections of what has long been the "standard social science model."[8] By this, I mean a set of explanations that tend to be parsimonious, attributing human behavior to one or two basic "causes" without recognizing that people often do things for complicated combinations of reasons. They tend to be static, neglecting the possibility that human behavior, individually or collectively, might change over time. They tend to claim universal applicability, thereby failing to acknowledge that different cultures—to say nothing of different individuals—respond to similar situations in different ways.[9] And they have, over the past century, differentiated social science from the field within which several of its major disciplines originated, which is history.[10]

So why have social scientists made these assumptions of parsimony, stability, and universality, when even to enumerate them is to suggest their problematic character? They've done so, I believe, for a specific reason: if they were to allow for multiple causes, or for the passage of time, or for cultural and individual diversity, explanations would proliferate and forecasting would become difficult if not impossible.[11] Were social scientists to proceed in this manner, they'd be functioning like historians, who gleefully proliferate variables all the time.

We're able to do that, though, because we concern ourselves only with phenomena that have passed through the singularity that separates the past from the future, which has in turn bound continuities and contingencies together for us. No one expects us to unzip this binding, like some DNA molecule seeking to replicate itself. No one demands that we forecast how such molecules might recombine in the future. "The historian's business is to know the past, not to know the future," R. G. Collingwood insisted, "and whenever historians claim to be able to determine the future in advance of its happening, we may know with certainty that something has gone wrong with their fundamental conception of history."[12] Or, as Tom Stoppard's heroine Thomasina puts it in his play *Arcadia*: "You cannot stir things apart."[13]

Historians are, as a consequence, in much less demand than social scientists when it comes to making recommendations for future policy. We have the consolation in contrast to them, though, of more often getting things right.

III.

Most of us have had the experience of being told, as students in first-year physics classes seeking to demonstrate Newton's laws of motion, not to worry about friction, or air resistance, or other inconveniences whose effects would be difficult to calculate. Instead we were supposed to visualize ideal pendulums swinging in perfect vacuums, featureless balls rolling down impossibly smooth inclined planes, and feathers and stones that always fell to earth at the same rate—even if our eyes told us that things never quite happened that way.

We were taught to make these assumptions to facilitate calculation: it was too hard to measure the effects of friction or air resistance, or to predict the variations in the results these might cause with each repeated experiment. So we were instructed just to "smooth out the data" until they illustrated the basic law of physics that was being demonstrated. It didn't matter if the actual results were a little messy: what was important was to understand the underlying principles.[14]

But look what was happening here: the requirement to be "scientific" meant that we were asked to reject what our own powers of observation were telling us. It drove us toward a Platonic realm of ideal forms that had little to do with the real world. It didn't come close to predicting the actual arrival, on the floor or on our feet, of those feathers and stones we kept being told to drop. One of the basic *techniques* of science, calculation, had taken precedence over one of the basic *objectives* of science, which is anticipating what's actually going to happen. The forecasts that emerged from this process, predictably enough, never quite worked out.

Much the same happened with social science forecasting, and for similar reasons. Actual economic and political history is filled with examples of people making irrational rather than rational choices on the basis of inaccurate rather than accurate information.[15] Sociologists themselves have questioned structural functionalism because of its bias in favor of social stability and its failure to explain social change.[16] Modernization theory vastly oversimplified what was happening in Asia, Africa, and Latin America during the Cold War, while providing a pseudo-scientific justification for Washington's foreign policy objectives.[17] Organizational history shows repeated instances of bureaucracies and the bureaucrats that run them acting in ways that don't perpetuate their interests.[18] Freudian psychology offers a less than adequate explanation of human behavior, especially when it's projected across cultures and through time, or when it's compared with physiological explanations.[19] And, of course, international relations theory, which organized itself around the study of power, failed utterly to explain why the two most powerful nations of the modern era chose, at certain points during the twentieth century, to relinquish power rather than retain it: the United States in 1919–20 and the Soviet Union in 1989–91.[20]

Students in the social sciences are often told to proceed "as if" these anomalies had not happened. Saving the *theory* is what's important: it doesn't matter if doing so "smooths out," or even flattens, the facts.[21] What this means, though, is that the social sciences are operating—by no means in all instances, but in many—at roughly the level of freshman physics experiments. That's why the forecasts they make only occasionally correspond with the reality we subsequently encounter.

Social scientists seem to have concluded that the only way they can both explain the past and anticipate the future is to imitate the laboratory sciences, with their capacity to rerun experiments, vary the parameters, and thereby establish hierarchies of causation. They feel that they've not done their job until they've separated independent from dependent variables. But they do so only by separating these variables from the world that surrounds them.[22]

The consequence is a methodological Catch-22. Social scientists seek to build universally applicable generalizations about necessarily simple matters; but if these matters were any more complicated, their theories wouldn't be universally applicable. Hence, when social scientists are right, they too often confirm the obvious. When they don't confirm the obvious, they're too often wrong.[23]

IV.

But is reductionism the *only* method we have of explaining the past and forecasting the future? To answer this question, let me return to the natural sciences, but this time to the ones like astronomy, geology, and paleontology that, because of their scope and scale, cannot confine themselves to laboratories. Or, as I put it in the last chapter, to those sciences that rely upon *virtual* rather than *actual* replicability as the means of verification.

It's certainly possible to know the direction in which galaxies are moving, or continents are drifting, or species are evolving. Yet these forecasts derive from a knowledge of systems: from a sense of how the parts interact to form the whole, not from a focus on the parts at the expense of the whole. Theories like relativity, plate tectonics, and natural selection emphasize relationships *among* variables, some of them continuous and others contingent. Regularity and randomness coexist within such theories: they allow for punctuations that upset equilibria, such as asteroid impacts, earthquakes, or the outbreak of new and lethal diseases.[24] Nor do they require singling out certain variables as more important than others: what would the independent variables be for the Andromeda galaxy, or the Norwegian coastline, or the Darwin finch?[25] Reductionism in these realms is only a stepping stone toward synthesis. It's not an end—or a method—in itself.

These disciplines work, as we've already seen, by deriving processes from structures, by fitting representations to realities, by privileging neither induction nor deduction, by remaining open—the word is *consilience*—to what insights from one field can tell you about another. And yet there's a directionality in all of them that allows us to make sense of the past and still in a very general way to anticipate the future. They meet the test of what a science should do, which is to explain, forecast, *and* generate a consensus as to the validity of the results. Can such an ecological approach work, though, within the field of human affairs?

Some social scientists have begun to explore this possibility. The growing "constructivist" movement in political science stresses the *evolution* of ideas and institutions: as in the natural sciences, Alexander Wendt explains, the emphasis is on "explaining why one thing leads to another, and how . . . things are put together to have the causal powers that they do."[26] The "new historicism" in sociology questions the tendency to seek universal generalizations detached from time and space.[27] "Behavioralist" economists are challenging the habit, particularly evident in their field, of valuing models over evidence.[28] And, inspired largely by the work of Alexander George, international relations theorists have begun to embrace the techniques of comparative case studies, which resist reductionism while encouraging an ecological perspective.[29]

Nevertheless, reductionism remains the dominant mode of inquiry within the social sciences: historians are still the principal practitioners of an ecological approach to the study of human affairs. To see why, it's worth exploring in greater detail the relationship between explanation and generalization as historians and social scientists have traditionally understood it.

V.

It's quite wrong to claim that historians reject the use of theory, for theory is ultimately generalization, and without generalization historians would have nothing whatever to say. The very words we use generalize complex realities—for example, "past," "present," and "future"—and we could hardly do without them.[30] We do, however, normally *embed our generalizations within our narratives*. In seeking to show how past processes have produced present structures, we draw upon whatever theories we can find that will help us accomplish that task. Because the past is infinitely divisible, we have to do this if we're to make sense of whatever portion of it we're attempting to explain. Explanation is, however, our chief priority: therefore we subordinate our generalizations to it. We're interested, as E. H. Carr put it, "in what is general in the unique."[31] We generalize for particular purposes; hence we practice *particular generalization*.

Social scientists, in contrast, tend to *embed narratives within generalizations*. Their principal objective is to confirm or refute a hypothesis, and they subordinate narration to that task. "Disaggregated data, or observations from a different time period, or even from a different part of the world, may provide additional observable implications of a theory," three distinguished practitioners acknowledge. "We may not be interested at all in these subsidiary implications, but if they are consistent with the theory, as predicted, they will help us build confidence in the power and applicability of the theory."[32] Theory therefore comes first, with explanation enlisted as needed to confirm it. Social scientists particularize for general purposes; hence they practice *general particularization*.[33]

This distinction between embedded and encompassing theory—between generalization lodged within time and generalization for all time—causes historians to function differently from their social science colleagues in several important ways:

Historians work with limited, not universal, generalizations. We rarely claim applicability for our findings beyond specific times and places. So although I argued, in *We Now Know*, that the structure of the Stalinist dictatorship rendered it insensitive to the impact of its actions beyond its borders, that's not an assertion I'd want to try to defend for *all* dictatorships. Nor, despite my claim that Stalin did just this, would I insist that dictators *always* project their domestic behavior onto the world at large.[34]

Such generalizations don't have to be universal, though, to have wide applicability. Historians are prepared to acknowledge tendencies, or patterns: these are certainly not laws applying in all instances, but they're certainly not useless either. If we had to make all of our judgments about reality only on the basis of laws, we'd be—because there're so few such laws—quite out of touch with most of reality. Anyone seeking to establish "the permanent and unchanging laws of human nature," Collingwood warns, is bound to have mistaken "the transient conditions of a certain historical age for the permanent conditions of human life."[35]

My generalization about Stalin might thus provide some basis for making comparisons to other dictatorships, or to democracies, or to still other forms of government.[36] It surely caused me to reconsider a proposition I'd absorbed long ago from "realist" theorists of international relations: that democracies have greater difficulties than autocracies in aligning their policies with their interests.[37] But would my amended hypothesis then apply, say, to China in the post–Cold War era? Here I and most other historians would hedge, echoing what Zhou Enlai is alleged to have said about the French Revolution: "It's too soon to say."

Historians believe in contingent, not categorical, causation. "It all depends," we'd continue, before holding forth on all that the future of China (or whatever else *it* might be) is likely to depend upon. As the philosopher Michael Oakeshott pointed out, historians have a web-like sense of reality, in that we see everything as connected in some way to everything else.[38] For that reason, it's not clear to us how any variable can be truly independent.

That doesn't mean, though, that we feel obliged to trace each causal chain back to the Big Bang. The further in the past a process lies, the less weight historians tend to give it in explaining resulting structures. Stalin could hardly have collectivized agriculture in the Soviet Union had prehistoric peoples not domesticated crops and animals several thousand years earlier, but historians of collectivization feel little need to make that point.[39] We separate out distinctive from routine links in causal relationships: in accounting for what happened at Hiroshima on August 6, 1945, we attach greater importance to the fact that President Truman ordered the dropping of an atomic bomb than to the decision of the Army Air Force to carry out his orders.[40] We try to identify points of "sensitive dependence on initial conditions" at which particular actions had larger consequences than might otherwise have been expected: hence the way in which a quarrel over the key to the Church of the Nativity in Bethlehem led—or so the historian Trevor Royle has argued—to the outbreak of the Crimean War.[41]

Historians reject, however, the doctrine of immaculate causation, which seems to be implied in the idea that one can identify, without reference to all that has preceded it, such a thing as an independent variable. Causes always have antecedents. We may rank their relative significance, but we'd think it irresponsible to seek to isolate—or "tease out"—single causes for complex events. We see history as proceeding instead from multiple causes and their intersections. Interconnections matter more to us than does the enshrinement of particular variables.[42] It follows, then, that:

Historians prefer simulations to modeling. Social scientists try to reduce the number of variables with which they deal because this facilitates calculation, which in turn simplifies the task of forecasting. But if events have complex causes, forecasting based on simple ones isn't likely to work particularly well.[43] Knowing this, historians prefer to avoid forecasting altogether, which frees us to incorporate as many variables as we want into our "retrocasting." There's a deeper issue here, though, which gets back to the point that although the past is never completely knowable, it is more knowable than the future.

Recounting the past requires narrative—*simulating* what happened—but not necessarily modeling. A simulation, as I'm using the term, attempts to illustrate (not replicate) some specific set of past events. A model seeks to show how a system has worked in the past but also how it will work in the future. Simulations need not forecast; models must. That's why models depend on parsimony, for when systems become complex, variables proliferate and forecasting becomes impossible: *systems themselves become entangled in events*. Parsimony, therefore, is a life preserver for social scientists: it keeps them from drowning in complexity.[44] Historians, who swim in that medium, have little need of it.

Historians trace processes from a knowledge of outcomes. Political scientists have begun using the term "process tracing" in recent years, which suggests a rediscovery of narrative; and the technique does indeed employ narratives in constructing comparative case studies. As Andrew Bennett and Alexander George have pointed out, however, process tracing seeks "not only to explain specific cases but also to test and refine theories, to develop new theories, and to produce generic knowledge of a given phenomenon." Because process tracing "converts a historical narrative into an *analytical* causal explanation . . . , [it] is substantially different from historical explanation."[45] However carefully it represents the past, therefore, process tracing still seeks to forecast the future. Historical explanation need not do so.

One might think, at first glance, that the first approach would be the more "scientific," since we've traditionally expected science to produce forecasts. But when you're working with multiple intersecting variables over long periods of time, the conditions that prevail at the beginning of a process guarantee very little about its end. "Alter any early event, ever so slightly," the paleontologist Stephen Jay Gould has written of his field, "and the evolution cascades into a radically different channel." This is not to say that the history of life—or, by implication, history in general—lacks patterns: "the divergent route . . . would be just as interpretable, just as explainable *after* the fact, as the actual road. But the diversity of possible itineraries does demonstrate that eventual results cannot be predicted at the outset."[46]

Historians generalize, therefore, but only from the knowledge of particular outcomes: that's what I mean by particular generalization. We derive processes from surviving structures; but because we understand that a shift in those processes at any point could have produced a different structure, we make few if any claims about the future. For historians, generalization doesn't normally mean forecasting. For social scientists, however, it often does: process tracing is meant to *anticipate* outcomes. Generalization does involve forecasting: it's generalized particularization. They're two quite different projects, in the end. But they're both scientific.[47]

VI.

This distinction between these two approaches became an important one for me in writing Cold War history. Like many other students of international relations, I'd been impressed by Kenneth Waltz's counterintuitive proposition (to me, at least), that bipolar systems are inherently more stable than multipolar systems.[48] The more I thought about this the more sense it made, and it was Waltz's insight that largely propelled me toward one of my own, which was that the rivalry between the United States and the Soviet Union had gradually evolved into a "long peace."[49] This was, I can now see, an example of embedded theory, or particular generalization: I used Waltz's "neorealism" to explain a particular historical outcome. But I didn't try to encompass the entire Cold War within a neorealist framework.

Waltz, however, did attempt that feat, and on the basis of such generalized particularization he made a forecast, in 1979, of how the Cold War would end. Soviet-American hostility would gradually diminish, he argued, but bipolarity would survive: "the barriers to entering the superpower club have never been higher and more numerous. The club will long remain the world's most exclusive one."[50] Waltz was quickly proven wrong on both counts: distrust between Washington and Moscow reached dangerous new levels during the early 1980s; but by the end of that decade bipolarity had virtually disappeared.

The problem here was Waltz's reductionism: his definition of power that accorded primacy to military capabilities; his insistence on sharp distinctions between system- and unit-level phenomena; and his aspiration to universality, which obscured the role the passage of time itself can play in determining the course of events.[51] For it's clear in retrospect that one of the most significant patterns in Cold War history was that of asymmetrically evolving capabilities: although both the United States and the Soviet Union began their rivalry possessing power in multiple dimensions—military power to be sure, but also ideological, economic, and even moral power—only the United States and its allies retained that multidimensionality, and with it the capacity to compete in a shifting international environment.[52] In order to anticipate the Cold War's outcome, therefore, we'd have needed a theory that addressed these different kinds of power as well as the environments within which they manifest themselves.

Might that have been possible? I think so, but I know of no one who attempted it. All of which leads me to the following retrospective passage about the end of the Cold War from *We Now Know*, which I wish I'd had the insight and imagination to write as a forecast a decade earlier in *The Long Peace*:

> To visualize what happened, imagine a troubled triceratops. From the outside, as rivals contemplated its sheer size, tough skin, bristling armament, and aggressive posturing, the beast looked sufficiently formidable that none dared tangle with it. Appearances deceived, though, for within its digestive, circulatory, and respiratory systems were slowly clogging up, and then shutting down. There were few external signs of this until the day the creature was found with all four feet in the air, still awesome but now bloated, stiff, and quite dead. The moral of the fable is that armaments make impressive exoskeletons, but that a shell alone ensures the survival of no animal and no state.[53]

Now, obviously this is a metaphor, not a theory. But don't theories sometimes begin with metaphors? The political scientists I know speak often enough of billiard balls, dominos, bandwagons, rolling logs, prisoner's dilemmas, stag hunts, and chickens—a very eclectic metaphorical menagerie! Why, therefore, can't a dead dinosaur provide a basis for a reconceptualization of theory drawn, this time, not from physics, but from medicine?

VII.

The theory would be this: that the health and ultimately the survival of states depends upon their maintaining a combination of life-support systems in balance with one another, and with their external environment. If any one of them gets out of whack and nothing is done, its collapse can affect all the others. Treatment may require specialists, to be sure, but no specialist will succeed without taking into account the entire organism, its case history, and its surrounding ecosystem. Physicians, in short, may offer us as much as freshman physics laboratory assistants in seeking to understand international relations and the states that function within them.[54]

But that's only to bring us back around to narrative, for what do physicians do, in treating their patients, if not track multiple interrelated processes over time, recounting these for others as well as themselves so that all may benefit? Physicians generalize, but only on a limited basis, for they must allow for the particularities of their patients as well as those of the ills that beset them. No physician would want to treat the heart without considering what the effects might be on the blood vessels, the lungs, the kidneys, and the brain: even in an era of specialization, doctors must still maintain some sense of the patient as a whole. They'd certainly not rely upon a monodimensional explanation for illness or health, nor would they want to have to depend upon a single remedy. Nor would they exclude the role of time, both as an enemy and as an ally in the art of healing.[55]

Physicians deal, therefore, with the paradox of particular generalization all the time. So do paleontologists, but also evolutionary biologists, astronomers, cartographers, historians — indeed, I'd venture to say, most of us in most aspects of everyday life. All of which raises the question once again: where does the push for generalized particularization in the social sciences actually come from?

Perhaps professionalization has produced a Freudian "narcissism of minor differences": groups often define themselves in terms of what their neighbors aren't.[56] Perhaps it's a confusion of form with function: methodological purity sometimes takes precedence, in discussions of theory, over simple questions like "What is it for?" Perhaps it's a misunderstanding of how the "hard" sciences operate, for particular generalization abounds in many of these. Or perhaps it's just physics envy.

Whatever the explanation, the issues involved here get at the heart of what it means to be "scientific." It certainly means seeking "a consensus of rational opinion over the widest possible field," as John Ziman has written.[57] But I think it also means connecting that consensus with the real world. When the only way you can get a consensus is to detach it from reality—when you value more highly the structure of your generalizations than the substance they convey—then it seems to me you risk a return to the kind of thinking that existed before the scientific revolutions of the seventeenth and eighteenth centuries, when the findings of Aristotle, or Galen, or Ptolemy were taken as authoritative despite the contradictory evidence that lay before everyone's eyes. As my former Yale colleague Rogers Smith has put it: "Elegance is not worth that price."[58]

Most natural scientists today would snort at the prospect of paying it. So too would most historians. But would social scientists? I can't help wondering whether the insistence on distinguishing independent from dependent variables has not become, within certain of the social sciences, a prescientific test of identity rather than a coherent method of inquiry. It seems to be one of the things you do to prove your credentials, to align yourself with orthodoxy, to show greater respect for authority than for reality.[59] But is there much beyond this that the technique accomplishes? If there isn't, then maybe "teasing out" should be left to a profession that could make better use of it. Like hairdressers.

Chapter Five

CHAOS AND COMPLEXITY

I CONCLUDED THE LAST CHAPTER with the suggestion — deliberately provocative, I'm afraid — that the methods of historians are closer to those of certain natural scientists than to those of most social scientists. The reason, I argued, is that too many social scientists, in their efforts to specify independent variables, have lost sight of a basic requirement of theory, which is to account for reality. They reduce complexity to simplicity in order to anticipate the future, but in doing so they oversimplify the past.

It's hardly surprising that these tendencies have placed the social scientists at odds with historians in general; and no doubt some social scientists will be especially at odds, when they read what I've written, with this historian in particular. But the social sciences have also diverged from the methods of those so-called "hard" scientists who don't rely solely, for the verification of findings, upon reproducible experimentation — in effect, the rerunning of time, the manipulation of variables this procedure allows, and their subsequent identification as either independent or dependent. Fields like astronomy, geology, paleontology, evolutionary biology, and medicine don't easily fit within the confines of laboratories. They necessarily concern themselves, as does history, with interdependent variables interacting in complicated ways over extended periods of time. And yet each of these sciences does, in its own way, tell us something about the future.

So can historians do that too? To begin to answer that question, I need to develop more fully the connections between history and "hard" science as they exist today. I'd like to begin with one historian's personal quest for the independent variable a century ago, and where that led him.

I.

The historian was our old friend Henry Adams, and the quest is chronicled in his extraordinary autobiography, *The Education of Henry Adams*, completed in 1907 but only published posthumously in 1918. Adams portrayed himself as seeking, throughout his life, some single "great generalization" that would provide the key to understanding the past and to forecasting the future. The historian's task, he wrote (using a surprisingly contemporary verb), "is to triangulate from the widest possible base to the furthest point he thinks he can see, which is always far beyond the curvature of the horizon."[1]

Was he serious? With Adams, it's always hard to tell. He was, at successive points in his career, both a "splitter" and a "lumper"—a master of excruciating detail, as in his great history of the Jefferson and Madison administrations, and yet also the most sweeping of synthesizers, as in his division of history into the ages, respectively, of the Virgin and the Dynamo.[2] To complicate matters further, Adams was fully capable of parodying both sides of himself. Still, few historians have written with greater insight about the search for independent variables in history, the difficulty of finding them, and the ways in which connections with "hard" science can demonstrate this.

Adams had been greatly impressed by such nineteenth-century scientific breakthroughs as "[t]he atomic theory; the correlation and conservation of energy; the mechanical theory of the universe; the kinetic theory of gases; and Darwin's Law of Natural Selection." The "great generalization" he hoped to find would be the equivalent for history—whether literally or metaphorically he never quite made clear. Invoking the analogy to magnetic fields, he claimed to be seeking the invisible lines of force that gave coherence to the past and that could be expected, therefore, to shape the future.[3]

A funny thing happened to Adams on the way to the future, though: he discovered chaos. The only "larger synthesis" that really worked, he came to believe, was one that didn't work at all, in the sense of providing an explanation of the past that would allow anticipating what was to come. Adams reached this conclusion by following the work of the French mathematician Henri Poincaré, who was doing pioneering research at the time on three-body problems and the equations with which to represent them. Poincaré showed that within such "dynamical" systems there was no clear relationship between independent and dependent variables; everything depended on everything else. Even if "our means of investigation should become more and more penetrating," he wrote, in a passage Adams quoted, "we should discover the simple under the complex; then the complex under the simple; then anew the simple under the complex; and so on without ever being able to foresee the last term." These findings, Adams remarked, "promised eternal bliss to the mathematician, but turned the historian green with horror."[4]

Poincaré's insights attracted relatively little attention over the next half century because he lacked the means of solving many of the complex equations these problems generated, or of representing the solutions visually.[5] With the development of computers, though, all of that changed, and the "new" sciences of chaos and complexity have arisen largely as a result. These raise the possibility, I think, of reviving Adams's old project, if not of discovering the nature of history, then at least of finding new terms with which to characterize its indeterminate workings. Not least among these is the phenomenon of *interde-*

pendent variables, or perhaps we might say complex as opposed to simple causation.

II.

Simple causation is easily understood. Changes in one variable produce corresponding changes in the others: x when it encounters y always results in z. The behavior of the system, therefore, is entirely predictable. A good example is the difference between driving from Oxford to London at 70 or 100 miles per hour. It's not at all difficult to figure out how much time you'll save—or how much more fuel you'll expend—by the angle you choose to maintain between your automobile's accelerator and its floor. In an ideal, uncluttered world, at least.

But the world is not ideal, the M-40 motorway is hardly uncluttered, and you can never really know in advance how long it's going to take you to drive from Oxford to London. For one thing, your chances of getting stopped by the police or of having an accident are considerably greater driving at 100 than at 70 miles per hour. If this happens to you—or if indeed something similar happens to any other of the tens of thousands of drivers who are trying to make their way down the M-40 on any weekday morning, or even if all that happens is that the tailgate on a single slow lorry comes loose, spilling some horrible substance like Marmite all over the roadway—then all bets are off, as is any hope of getting to London in time for your lecture or your job interview. You're into the realm of complex causation.

Each driver who sees the flashing blue lights of the police or the emergency vehicles will slow down accordingly, but not at the same rate. Soon there'll be a traffic backup extending for miles. This will result, however, not directly from the precipitating event, but rather from tens of thousands of individual decisions to hit or release the brakes, each of them made in relation to what all the other drivers are doing.

What's happening here is that predictable and unpredictable phenomena are occurring within the same system. The behavior of the drivers in our traffic tie-up is quite predictable. Most of them will slow down when they see the police or the ambulances, almost all of them will hit their brakes when they realize that the cars ahead of them are hitting theirs, and absolutely all of the Americans who happen to be driving that day will gag at the smell of Marmite. What's unpredictable is the aggregate behavior of all these drivers—the macro-effect that comes from their micro-responses.

For these micro-responses will not all have taken place in just the same way. The drivers' attentiveness will vary according to which of them had a rough night, or are talking on their cell phones. But even if everyone was paying the closest attention, reactions would still reflect differences in the vision and the reflexes of each driver, which in turn would depend upon the speed with which the necessary electrochemical impulses had crossed the required zillions of synapses, and so on. Multiply these by the number of drivers in our traffic jam, and you've got something approaching an infinite number of interdependent variables, no one of which is any more the cause of the problem than are any of the others.

The micro-level phenomena within our system are, for the most part, *linear* in character, in that there's a predictable relationship between input and output, between stimulus and response. Indeed without such linearity and the generalizations it makes possible—for example, that drivers tend to hit their brakes when they see red lights ahead—the task of simple narration would overwhelm us: we'd have to account for each of the relevant rough nights, cell phones, reflexes, and nerve impulses. We'd be far worse off than we were, in a previous chapter, with Napoleon's underwear. We get around this by practicing *particular generalization*: we assume things that would otherwise bog us down. Without such a procedure we'd have no hope of representing the past, because the alternative would be to replicate the past, an obvious impossibility.

But the macro-level behavior of our system as a whole—the M-40 on the day of our traffic jam—is *non-linear*. Relationships do exist between input and output, between stimulus and response, but there are so many of these variables and they are all so interdependent that we can't possibly calculate their effects ahead of time. As the playwright Tom Stoppard has explained the mathematics, you're feeding the solution back into the equation and solving it, over and over again. It happens in any system "which eats its own numbers—measles epidemics, rainfall averages, cotton prices, it's a natural phenomenon in itself. Spooky."[6] For this reason, *generalized particularization*—the application of some general theory of traffic jams to this particular one—isn't likely to tell us much about what we really want to know, which is how much longer we're going to have to sit in it.[7]

Poincaré's great insight was to show that linear and non-linear relationships could coexist: that the same system can be simple and complex at the same time. Adams saw the connection to history and threw up his hands, failing to understand how such a monstrosity could ever be characterized in the scientific terms with which he was familiar. What Adams didn't foresee was that Poincaré's work would point the way toward a new kind of science: one that distinguishes between the predictable and the non-predictable, that doesn't depend upon reducing complexity to simplicity, that acknowledges—indeed relishes—the interdependency of variables; a science, in short, that's much like history.

III.

There is, in one sense, nothing new about chaos and complexity, if by these terms you mean acknowledging indeterminacy. For just as the social sciences were attempting to prove their legitimacy by moving *toward* the predictability that had characterized physics since the days of Isaac Newton—the methods Adams had hoped to apply to history—the physicists themselves were moving *away* from that approach. William H. McNeill has described the process: "[T]he old certainties of the Newtonian world machine, with its impressive capability of predicting and retrodicting the motions of sun, moon, planets, and even comets unexpectedly dissolved into an evolving, historical, and occasionally chaotic universe."[8] There occurred, in short, a methodological passing of ships in the night.

If Poincaré's equations horrified Adams, what would he have made of Einstein or Heisenberg? For if conceptions of time and space were themselves relative, if the observation of phenomena itself distorted phenomena, then it was difficult to see how historians or anyone else could achieve certainty: what you saw, and therefore what you thought, depended in the most literal possible sense on where you stood. Physics offered little basis for thinking you could triangulate the future, because there was no way to be sure that you'd correctly triangulated the past.

Nor could even continuity be taken for granted. The old scientific view had been that change was gradual or "uniformitarian" in rate, and hence a kind of system in itself.[9] Aware that history had been full of abrupt shifts and catastrophic events, Adams had himself doubted this proposition, but hadn't pursued the matter.[10] During the twentieth century, though, the "hard" sciences came to doubt it too: witness the realization that electrons can jump instantaneously from one orbit around the atomic nucleus to another; or what Thomas Kuhn has taught us about scientific revolutions and the "paradigm shifts" that accompany them;[11] or the work of Stephen Jay Gould and Niles Eldridge on "punctuated equilibrium" in the evolution of species;[12] or—most dramatically—the findings of Luis Alvarez and others about asteroid impacts and species annihilation.[13]

What came out of all of this was the realization, not just in physics but also in chemistry, geology, zoology, paleontology, and even astronomy, that Poincaré had been right: some things are predictable and some are not; regularities coexist with apparent randomness; both simplicity and complexity characterize the world in which we live. Even before chaos and complexity theory began to emerge in the 1970s, then, the old scientific perspective, in which one could assume the absolute nature of time and space, objectivity in observation, predictable rates of change—and therefore distinctions between dependent and independent variables—was about as outdated in the natural sciences as the Ptolemaic model of the universe had been in Newton's day.[14]

Chaos and complexity theory extended these insights in three ways: by clarifying the circumstances in which the predictable becomes unpredictable; by showing that patterns can still exist when there appear to be none; and by demonstrating that these patterns can emerge spontaneously, without anyone having put them there. Together, these findings enhance our understanding of the difference between linear and non-linear relationships—how orderly systems can become disorderly, or the other way around. These are useful things for historians to know about, since they have to grapple with such questions all the time.

But chaos and complexity offer something else that's at least as important for historians. They provide ways of visually representing relationships between predictable and non-predictable phenomena that in precomputer days could only have been expressed in forbiddingly difficult mathematics. They therefore give us *a new kind of literacy*, and hence a new set of terms for representing historical processes.[15] Let me be very clear: these are metaphors. They aren't those processes themselves. But when you remember that Adams too was relying on metaphors to represent historical processes—hence his use of the Virgin and the Dynamo to symbolize the shift from a religious to a secular consciousness—then the connections become intriguing.

So what might Henry Adams have done with chaos, complexity, and a computer? There follow some speculative suggestions, which I'll try to use in turn to clarify my larger point about how historians deal with interdependent variables.

IV.

Sensitive dependence on initial conditions. During the 1960s the meteorologist Edward Lorenz set out to model weather patterns on a primitive computer. He built in twelve parameters, allowed his program to run over several simulated days, and expected to find linear relationships between input and output that would improve the accuracy of forecasting. Instead what he got were widely varying results at the end stemming from tiny shifts—the difference, for example, between figures carried to three and six decimal places—in the data he had entered at the beginning. Since real weather conditions could never be measured even with this degree of precision, Lorenz concluded that forecasting in this field would always remain problematic: theoretically, at least, the fluttering of a butterfly's wings over Beijing could cause a hurricane to hit Baltimore.[16]

Historians will recognize here a reformulation of the famous "Cleopatra's nose" hypothesis: that if the object in question had been of a slightly different shape, its owner would not have been as attractive to Julius Caesar and Marc Antony, and the subsequent history of the world would have been different. David Hackett Fischer has objected rather literally to this proposition, pointing out that "[s]urely other anatomical parts were more important to a red-blooded Roman."[17] But beyond jokes of this nature—and predictable recitations about nails, horseshoes, and lost kingdoms—historians have had no very good basis for thinking seriously about how small events can produce big consequences, even as they've acknowledged the ubiquity of the problem.

The issue is: how do you know such an event when you see one? Why shouldn't Cleopatra's elbow have led to the rise and fall of empires? How is it that the dropping of a single grain of sand can cause a sand pile to collapse, when millions have preceded it without producing such an effect?[18] Lorenz's computer model provides an answer to such questions, which is that in complex systems you can never sort out critical variables in advance. You can only attempt to specify them in retrospect, and that's tough enough to do.

The word "complex" here has nothing to do with the size of the system in question. The M-40 is a complex system because so many variables interact within it. So too, as anyone who lives there quickly discovers, is the weather over Oxfordshire. But the motion of a spacecraft beyond earth orbit is relatively simple: as a result, it's easier to estimate arrival times on Mars than in London, and you might as well lug your umbrella around Oxford whatever the forecast has said.[19]

Systems with small numbers of variables therefore lend themselves to modeling. Systems with many variables don't: the only way you can explain their behavior is to simulate them, which means to trace their history. Natural scientists have certainly noticed this, and not just with respect to the weather. They know how difficult it is to specify at what point sand will slide, or what the shape of a snowflake will be, or when an earthquake will occur.[20] Gould has gone so far as to rewrite the history of life in these terms, challenging the old idea of the survival of the fittest by suggesting instead that contingency—which organisms lucked into hospitable evolutionary niches—played the decisive role. Rerunning the tape, were that possible, would produce different results; only historical investigation, therefore, can account for what actually happened. "The appropriate methods focus on narrative," he insists, "not experiment as usually conceived."[21]

This is what social scientists mean when they use the term "path dependency": a small event at the beginning of a process makes a big difference at the end of it.[22] The economists Paul David and Brian Arthur, for example, have shown that technologies evolve less from rational choices made on the basis of perfect information than from historical accidents: which innovations caught on first. Their most

famous illustration is the typewriter keyboard, whose now inescapable
QWERTY configuration is hardly the optimal arrangement for such a
device.[23] The political scientist Robert Putnam, curious as to why certain Italian regions today have governments that work while others
don't, found the best explanation to be historical: which city-states
had strong civic consciousness five or more centuries ago.[24] The terms
"constructivism," "behaviorialism," and "historicism," as they're coming to be used in political science, economics, and sociology, reflect
the importance of path dependency: they provide a theoretical basis
for taking history seriously.[25]

But insights like these raise serious difficulties for forecasting,
because, as Gould suggests, rerunning the tape in such complex systems would never produce the same outcome. Any reliance on reductionism to simplify the past in order to anticipate the future becomes
unworkable in these situations, and we're back to the old-fashioned
historical narrative. So what does a term like *sensitive dependence on
initial conditions* really tell us? Only, I think, that we should gain a
new appreciation of narrative as a more sophisticated research tool
than most social scientists—indeed than most historians—have yet
realized.

V.

Fractals. I've already mentioned Lewis Richardson's famous question
"How long is the coastline of Britain?" The answer, of course, is that it
depends on the units with which you calculate it: measurement in
terms of miles, kilometers, meters, feet, inches, and centimeters
would all produce different results, and the same problem would presumably extend down to the levels of molecules and atoms.[26]

The versatile Yale mathematician Benoit Mandelbrot has taken this
problem one step further, however, to show that there's another kind of
measurement you can perform on the British coastline that will give

you a single answer: it has to do with the degree of irregularity itself, or how crinkled it is. When you apply the principles of "fractal" geometry—Mandelbrot's term—in nature, a surprising phenomenon emerges: it's that of self-similarity across scale. The degree of roughness or smoothness, of complexity or simplicity, is often the same whether you're observing from a microscopic or a macroscopic perspective, or anywhere in between.

If you pull a cauliflower apart into smaller and smaller pieces, the shapes remain similar. Something like this also happens when you zoom in on blood vessels, electrical discharges, cracks in pavement, and even the shapes of mountains on near and distant horizons. The drainage patterns you see in an airplane from thirty thousand feet up resemble the tree branches you might see from thirty feet below them. Patterns tend to remain the same, in such systems, regardless of the scale at which one looks at them.[27]

© Bill Ross / CORBIS. © Bill Ross / CORBIS.
© Wayne Lawler; Ecoscene / CORBIS. © Anthony Cooper; Ecoscene / CORBIS.

Four fractals, the two on the top computer generated,
the two on the bottom natural.

Fractals, as Tom Stoppard's nineteenth-century heroine Thomasina explains in *Arcadia*, are "a method whereby all the forms of nature must give up their numerical secrets and draw themselves through numbers alone." Hannah, one of the twentieth-century characters in the play, then picks up an apple leaf:

HANNAH: So you couldn't make a picture of this leaf by iterating a whatsit?

VALENTINE: Oh yes, you could do that. . . . If you knew the algorithm and fed it back say ten thousand times, each time there'd be a dot somewhere on the screen. You'd never know where to expect the next dot. But gradually you'd start to see this shape, because every dot will be inside the shape of this leaf. It wouldn't *be* a leaf, it would be a mathematical object. But yes. The unpredictable and the predetermined unfold together to make everything the way it is.[28]

And what are the implications for history? Well, start with a single sentence from E. H. Carr: "It does not follow that, because a mountain appears to take on different shapes from different angles of vision, it has objectively either no shape at all or an infinity of shapes."[29] Carr used this insight to attack relativism: the argument that there's no objectivity in history, and that any historian's interpretation is as valid as anyone else's. What it suggests to me, though, is that, without having a word for what he was describing, Carr instinctively understood the concept of fractal geometry and saw its connection to history. Nor was he unique in this.

We've already seen Macaulay, Adams, and McNeill, in their great histories, zooming in and out between macroscopic and microscopic perspectives: what links these together is a kind of self-similarity across scale.[30] Michel Foucault built an entire career demonstrating that patterns of authority remain much the same whether at the level of discourse, families, cities, institutions, states, nations, or cultures.[31] Studies of dictatorships show behavior at the top spawning similar behavior down through regional, local, and even neighborhood institutions: it's difficult to read the remarkable diaries of Victor Klemperer, for example, without seeing Hitler's anti-Semitism extending itself throughout the levels of Nazi German society into the most mundane aspects of everyday life.[32]

But fractals could also provide a metaphor, I think, for movement in the other direction: for behavior that emerges spontaneously at the bottom, and gradually makes its way to the top. The reaction against authoritarianism during the second half of the twentieth century would certainly qualify, as would computer literacy, the Internet,[33] and certain otherwise inexplicable developments in popular culture. As for example how it happened that Elvis is still sighted regularly, or that a Beatle wound up as a knight.

VI.

Self-organization. This phenomenon has given both "hard" scientists and social scientists a good deal of trouble over the years. Physicists have long regarded as universally applicable the Second Law of Thermodynamics, which states that everything in the universe tends toward entropy, or "heat death"; but this principle seems hard to reconcile with the tendency of certain life forms, as they evolve, to become more complex.[34] Social scientists, confronting apparently anarchic phenomena like markets or the international state system, have encountered similar difficulties in explaining how cooperation can evolve within such structures.[35]

But the chaos theorists have shown, in the physical world, that surprising patterns of regularity can exist within what appear to be chaotic systems. The classic example is the Great Red Spot on Jupiter, which has retained its shape and size for as long as we've been able to see that planet's surface, despite its otherwise turbulent atmosphere. Certain non-linear equations, when plotted on computer screens, produce "strange attractors," which confine unpredictable processes within predictable structures.[36] Students of complexity, using computer modeling, have shown that organized behavior can emerge spontaneously in simulations in which units are allowed to interact with one another according to only a few basic rules.[37]

All of this has led to a growing interest in complex adaptive systems.[38] How is it that flocks of birds or schools of fish all know when to turn at the same time? What accounts for stock market booms and busts? Why do great empires gradually arise, exert their influence, and then suddenly and unexpectedly disintegrate? How, for that matter, could the Cold War have evolved into a Long Peace?[39]

Historians, of course, have long concerned themselves with the interactive behavior of masses, institutions, and individuals. Traditional social science, with its emphasis on seeking out independent variables, has given us few tools with which to understand such relationships. But the natural sciences are producing interesting insights from which both historians and social scientists might benefit. Two in particular are worth mentioning.

One of these has to do with a remarkably simple pattern that underlies complexity across a wide range of phenomena: it's the ubiquity of power-law relationships. The idea here is that the frequency of events is inversely proportional to their intensity. That sounds pretty abstract, until you put it in terms of earthquakes. There are, it turns out, several hundred of these in California each day. The vast majority, however, are imperceptible, falling within category three or below on the well-known Richter scale, in which the numbers go up by one as the intensity goes up by ten. Category four and five earthquakes, which you can feel but which do little or no damage, are fortunately less frequent, and it's even more fortunate that the really damaging earthquakes are the rarest of all. The pattern is sufficiently consistent that it can be expressed mathematically: double the energy released in the earthquake, and it becomes roughly four times as rare.[40]

What's interesting about this is that the same power-law relationship seems to apply—as if it were a fractal—across a surprisingly wide range of phenomena extending from species annihilations and forest fires to stock market crashes and war casualties. There is, apparently, a common structure underlying at least a sufficient variety of physical, biological, and human phenomena that Adams might well have regarded it—had he known about it—as his "great generalization." What connects these phenomena is that they're all in something other than a state of equilibrium: the new word for this is *criticality*, which simply means that a system contains within it both sensitive dependence on initial conditions and self-similarity across scale. The possibility therefore exists for an abrupt transition from one phase to another, and the likelihood of that happening is inversely proportional to the magnitude of the event when it occurs.[41]

Can we detect criticality in history? Of course we can in retrospect: that's what we're doing when we trace the rise and fall of empires, the beginnings and the endings of wars, the diffusion of ideas and technologies, the outbreaks of plagues and famines, perhaps even the emergence and disappearance of "great" men and women whose qualifications for "greatness" depend upon their capacity to influence others.[42] Whether we can forecast criticality is another matter, however, depending on what we understand the word "forecasting," in this context, to mean.

If it means anticipating relationships between intensity and frequency—the workings of the power-law—then we probably can do this, in a very crude way: the greater the intensity the lesser the frequency, by a factor we should be capable of calculating. But if it means anticipating *when* a particular situation is going to reach a condition of maximum intensity—a catastrophic war, for example, or a teeth-rattling revolution—then almost certainly we can't: the intersecting variables can only be reconstructed in retrospect. If, however, we're trying to determine who is likely to survive such upheavals and possibly even benefit from them, then there's at least some reason to think this feasible, based on the other major insight that's emerged from the work of natural scientists on self-organization.

It's the suggestion that survivors tend to be those organisms that are required to adapt frequently—but not too frequently—to the unexpected. A controlled environment is bad because you become complacent, set in your ways, and unable to cope when the controls finally do break down, as they ultimately will. But a completely unpredictable environment allows too little room for consolidation and recuperation. There is, thus, a balance between integrative and disintegrative processes in the natural world—the edge of chaos, so to speak—which is where innovation, especially through self-organization, normally occurs.[43]

It's no great stretch to suggest that something similar may work in the social, political, and economic world, for as McNeill has concluded, in an observation that would have fascinated Henry Adams: "*Surprising new forms of collective behavior arise from what appear to be spontaneous appearances of increasing levels of complexity, whether at the physical, chemical, biological, or symbolic levels. This strikes me as the principal unifying theme that runs through all we know, or think we know, about the world around us.*"[44]

VII.

In his useful book *Complexity*, M. Mitchell Waldrop describes a meeting between physicists and economists that took place at the Santa Fe Institute some years ago. I think it may stand as a symbolic turning point in the intellectual history of our times—rather in the way that Adams's encounter with Poincaré did a century ago:

[A]s the axioms and theorems and proofs marched across the overhead projection screen, the physicists could only be awestruck at [the economists'] mathematical prowess—awestruck and appalled. "They were almost too good," says one young physicist, who remembers shaking his head in disbelief. "It seemed as though they were dazzling themselves with fancy mathematics, until they really couldn't see the forest for the trees. So much time was spent on trying to absorb the mathematics that I thought they often weren't looking at what the models were for, and what they did, and whether the underlying assumptions were any good. In a lot of cases, what was required was just some common sense."[45]

Remember, this is a *physicist* talking about *economists*. What this anecdote suggests is something rather important: that the natural sciences changed dramatically during the twentieth century, even as the social scientists attempted to base much of what they did upon the sciences of the nineteenth and preceding centuries.[46]

So where does all of this leave the historians, who never bought into the standard social scientific model in the first place? It leaves us, I believe, in the curious position of having come out on the cutting edge of a revolution by persisting in a thoroughly reactionary stance. Without our having had to do anything different—indeed without even realizing, for the most part, what's happened—we find ourselves, at least in metaphorical terms, practicing the new sciences of chaos, complexity, and even criticality. We're like Molière's bourgeois gentleman, who was astonished to discover that he'd been speaking prose all his life.[47]

The connection Adams looked for between science and history now seems quite feasible, and in a way that does violence to the work of neither scientists nor historians. As in any complex adaptive system, both groups would benefit from the stimuli each could provide the other, not least because historians already know a lot about what the scientists are only now discovering to be one of the most sophisticated of all methods of inquiry: the narrative. And surely the social sciences—the last holdouts for the old scientific view—are going to have to adapt to this new environment if they're to continue to regard themselves as sciences at all.[48] Several of them are, quite literally, on the edge of chaos.

Historians are in a good position to serve as a bridge between the natural sciences on the one hand, and the social sciences on the other. But first we'll have to recognize the strategic position we occupy in the Great Interdisciplinary Chain of Being. Too few historians have noticed, McNeill points out, that

> our profession seems on the verge of becoming truly imperial— sharing perplexities and limitations with all the other branches of learning, even the most resolutely and successfully mathematical. For, insofar as historians focus attention on human behavior—and ecological historians are today extending their domain beyond that boundary—we can justly claim to address the most subtle and complex dimensions of the known and knowable universe.[49]

We can achieve that awareness only by looking outward rather than inward; and we've no reason, as we do so, to suffer from any kind of methodological inferiority complex. "Physics envy" need not be a problem for historians because—metaphorically at least—we've been doing a kind of physics all along.

Chapter Six

CAUSATION, CONTINGENCY, AND COUNTERFACTUALS

I'VE TRIED TO MAKE the case, in the last two chapters, that the search for independent variables in the social sciences can't succeed because the procedures upon which it depends are based on an out-moded view of the so-called "hard" sciences. Social scientists during the twentieth century embraced a Newtonian vision of linear and therefore predictable phenomena even as the natural sciences were abandoning it. Hence, the methodological passing of ships in the night.

The historians, in contrast, have remained happily on their methodological island, going about their business largely unaffected by these trends, for the most part hardly even aware of them. Those few like Marc Bloch and E. H. Carr who bothered to scan the horizon saw the paradox: that the ship sailing toward the historians was that of the "hard" sciences, which don't deal with human affairs at all, while the one fading from view was the one that claimed, at least, to be building a science of society. But Bloch died—at the hands of the Gestapo, in France, in 1944—before he could expand this argument.[1] Carr had hoped to pursue it in a revised version of *What Is History?*, but left only fragmentary notes for such a project at the time of his death in 1982.[2]

Little has happened since to alter this situation. The social sciences and the "hard" sciences, even today, proceed from quite different views of what *science* is all about,[3] while the historians give little thought to whether they practice science at all and, if so, of what variety.[4] Like J.R.R. Tolkien's hobbits, they're for the most part content to remain where they are, and are not much interested in what goes on around them. Or so I've tried to argue so far.

The time has come now, though, to try to answer the question social scientists have every right to ask and no doubt will: if there really are only dependent variables in history, then how do historians establish and confirm causal relations among them? How, if everything depends upon everything else, can we ever know the cause of anything? Natural scientists too may find this problem puzzling. And although most historians instinctively know the answer, we rarely provide it. "Don't ask, we won't tell," we too often reply when our students ask about causation. "Just finish your thesis. We'll let you know when you've got it right."

I described this attitude in the preface as an anti–Pompidou Center aesthetic: the fact that historians don't like to display ductwork. Without some attention to such matters, however, we're apt to confuse not only our students but also ourselves. We mumble when the social scientists tell us we aren't really doing science. We grumble at the postmodernists who claim that what we're writing is only fiction. But we don't respond effectively to either argument. We therefore leave ourselves, hobbit-like, open to attack. And we miss out on the peculiar satisfaction—perhaps even a pardonable basis for self-congratulation—that could come from the belated discovery that our methods have been more sophisticated than our own awareness of them: that, as William H. McNeill has put it, our "practice has been better than [our] epistemology."[5]

I.

A good place to begin any discussion of causation and verification is where Carr and Bloch ended theirs: with dead bodies.[6] The corpse Carr described has become famous to students of historical methodology: it's that of the unfortunate Robinson, run down while crossing the road to purchase cigarettes by a drunken Jones, driving a car with defective brakes around a blind corner on a dark night. Carr used this case to distinguish between what he called "rational" and "accidental" causation:

> [I]t made sense to suppose that the curbing of alcoholic indulgence in drivers, or a stricter control over the condition of brakes, or an improvement in the siting of roads, might serve the end of reducing the number of traffic fatalities. But it made no sense at all to suppose that the number of traffic fatalities could be reduced by preventing people from smoking cigarettes.

Rational causes, Carr went on to explain, "lead to fruitful generalizations and lessons can be learned from them." Accidental causes "teach no lessons and lead to no conclusions." Historians, he insisted, need concern themselves only with the first category; the second had "no meaning, either for the past or the present."[7]

Carr thereby managed to confuse not only his readers but himself. Leave aside the two senses in which he uses the word "accident": as both a general set of causes and as a particular consequence. A more serious problem is the murkiness of his distinction between the "rational" and the "accidental." It's certainly rational to claim that Robinson's nicotine addiction led him on this particular night to cross this particular road in front of this particular automobile that Jones, owing to his alcohol addiction, was driving particularly badly. But here a series of rational causes combined to produce an accidental consequence: Carr's categories therefore blur, even within the case he chose to illustrate their distinctiveness.

The claim that accidents have no "meaning" in history is even less convincing, as Carr himself later admitted when pressed to explain how Lenin's fatal stroke had not altered the course of Soviet history.[8] What Carr appeared to be trying to say was that you can't predict such accidents; but this raises another question, which is whether historians should be attempting to make such predictions in the first place. Carr seemed to think they should: the whole point of specifying "rational" causes, he argued, was to provide "fruitful generalizations and lessons" that would, in turn, lead to "conclusions." He ducked the issue, though, of who's to teach such lessons, and how we'll know when they've got them right. It's an unsettling omission, given the frequency with which Carr himself got such lessons wrong.[9]

For all of these reasons, I prefer Marc Bloch's connection of causes with corpses: his example is that of a man falling to his death from a precipice. Many things had to have happened, Bloch pointed out, in order to produce this outcome: the man had to have slipped; the path he was walking along had to have been built along the edge of a cliff; geological processes had to have uplifted the mountain from the plain; the law of gravity had to have been in effect; and, Bloch might have added, the Big Bang had to have occurred. Still, anyone asked the cause of the accident would probably reply: "a misstep." The reason, Bloch explained, is that this particular antecedent differed from all the others in several ways: "it occurred last; it was . . . the most exceptional in the general order of things; [and] finally, by virtue of this greater particularity, it seems the antecedent which could have been most easily avoided."[10]

Bloch's actual death prevented him from discussing any more fully this hypothetical death, and, as a consequence, his thinking on causation is less well known than Carr's. Even in its fragmentary form, however, it goes well beyond Carr in its sophistication, consistency, and usefulness. For if I read Bloch correctly, he was suggesting three sets

of distinctions that have to be made in connecting causes with consequences: one between the immediate, the intermediate, and the distant; a second between the exceptional and the general; and a third
between the factual and the counterfactual. Let me expand on each of
these, attempting as I do so to show how they might relate, at least
metaphorically, to the "new" sciences of chaos and complexity.

II.

First, *the distinction between the immediate, the intermediate, and the
distant*. Although historical narratives normally move forward, historians in preparing them move backward.[11] They tend to start with some
particular phenomenon—large or small—and then trace its antecedents. Or, to put it in the terms I used earlier, they begin with structures and then derive the processes that produced them. In a tacit
acknowledgment of Bloch's mountain climber's misstep, they assign
the greatest importance to the most proximate of these processes—
but they don't stop there.

It would make no sense, for example, to begin an account of the
Japanese attack on Pearl Harbor with the launching of the planes
from their carriers: you'd want to know how the carriers came to be
within range of Hawaii, which requires explaining why the government in Tokyo chose to risk war with the United States. But you can't
do that without discussing the American oil embargo against Japan,
which in turn was a response to the Japanese takeover of French
Indochina. Which of course resulted from the opportunity provided
by France's defeat at the hands of Nazi Germany, together with the
frustrations Japan had encountered in trying to conquer China.
Accounting for all of this, however, would require some attention to
the rise of authoritarianism and militarism during the 1930s, which in
turn had something to do with the Great Depression as well as the
perceived inequities of the post–World War I settlement, and so on.

You could continue this process all the way back to the moment, hundreds of millions of years earlier, when the first Japanese island rose up, in great billowing clouds of steam and smoke, from what was to become the Pacific Ocean. However, we don't usually go back quite that far.

There's no precise rule that tells historians where to stop in tracing the causes of any historical event. But there is what we might call a *principle of diminishing relevance*: it is that the greater the time that separates a cause from a consequence, the less relevant we presume that cause to be. Notice that I didn't use the term "irrelevant," although Carr at one point did in dismissing what he called "accidental" causes.[12] The Japanese government could hardly have decided to attack the United States if the Japanese islands had never surfaced, any more than Bloch's mountain climber could have fallen if the mountain had never arisen. The relevance of these causes, however, is sufficiently remote that they don't tell us very much: to invoke them is like explaining the success of the Japanese fighter pilots in terms of the fact that prehumans evolved binocular vision and opposable thumbs. We expect the causes we cite to connect rather more directly to consequences. When they don't, we tend to disregard them.[13]

What about causes that are neither immediate nor distant but intermediate? The principle of diminishing relevance works here too, but the zone of "intermediacy" is sufficiently great that we need some additional standard for differentiating between low levels of relevance at one end of it and high levels at the other. In the Pearl Harbor case, for example, we might place the emergence of Shintoism, the Tokugawa ascendancy, and the Meiji Restoration within the first category, and the Great Depression, the rise of militarism, and the invasions of China and Indochina within the second. But what's happening when we make these kinds of judgments?

III.

It's here, I think, that Bloch's second distinction, between *exceptional* and *general* causes, comes into play. Bloch's point was that although his mountain climber could not have fallen from his precipice without the path along it having been built, without the mountain having been uplifted, and without the law of gravity having been in effect, not everyone who skirts precipices plummets from them. The placement of the path, the existence of the mountain, the effects of gravity were all general causes of the accident: they were *necessary* for the death to have occurred, but they weren't in themselves *sufficient* to explain it. For that, we have to come back to the misstep.

This distinction between necessary and sufficient causation isn't the same as the one between dependent and independent variables that social scientists like to make.[14] For a sufficient cause is still dependent upon necessary causes: that's why a misstep on a mountain path is more dangerous than one that takes place in the middle of a meadow. It would make no more sense to discuss either of these missteps without specifying where they occurred than it would to place the Japanese carriers off Hawaii without explaining how they got there. Causes always have contexts, and to know the former we must understand the latter.

Indeed I would go so far as to define the word "context" as the dependency of sufficient causes upon necessary causes; or, in Bloch's terms, of the exceptional upon the general. For while context does not directly *cause* what happens, it can certainly determine consequences. In the case of the missteps I've just mentioned, it makes the difference between (at worst, in the meadow) a broken ankle and (at best, from the precipice) a broken neck.

Bloch's understanding of exceptional causes, I think, anticipates what the chaos theorists have called "sensitive dependence on initial conditions," and Carr may have had something similar in mind when he spoke so confusingly about "accidental" causes. Neither historian lived long enough to hear about "butterfly effects"—the now famous butterfly over Beijing that wreaks such havoc elsewhere[15]—to say nothing of the very recently discovered Florida butterfly ballot. But like most historians Bloch and Carr seem instinctively to have known about such phenomena nonetheless, and to have been grasping for a way to characterize their workings.

How, though, do we know a moment of sensitive dependence—or of exceptional causation—when we come across one? Neither Bloch nor Carr has an answer for this, but physics may. For in that field it's done by looking for phase transitions, those points of criticality at which stability becomes unstable: where water begins to boil or freeze, for example, or sand piles begin to slide, or fault lines begin to fracture.[16] Much the same thing happens in evolutionary biology when the climate suddenly shifts, or when new predators are introduced, or when epidemics break out: the resulting instabilities give rise to new patterns of stability that can't be predicted in advance.[17] And in a computer program like the one through which Edward Lorenz first discovered sensitive dependence on initial conditions, the phase transition is the moment at which the program begins to run, when minute variations in some particular input can produce a wildly unpredictable output.[18]

Are there phase transitions in history? The historian Clayton Roberts, without actually using the term, seems to believe that there are. "Historians," he writes, "instinctively stop the backward search for the ultimate cause at the point where the state of affairs, whose alteration they seek to explain, flourished."[19] This is a rather clumsy way of stating, for history, a principle paleontologists have more elegantly called *punctuated equilibrium*. It has to do with the fact that evolution doesn't proceed at a steady rate; rather, long periods of stability are "punctuated" by abrupt and destabilizing changes. These tend to give rise to new species, whose origins paleontologists would trace back to the point of punctuation, but not to the beginnings of life itself, or to the Big Bang.[20]

Roberts is suggesting something like this, I think, in the way historians operate. We start with a particular event, whether it's the attack on Pearl Harbor or, in the example Roberts cites, the English Civil War. We work backward from it, assigning greater importance to immediate rather than distant causes. The further back we go, though, the more possible causes we're going to find. So if we're not to wind up rewriting the history of the Meiji Restoration or the Protestant Reformation—if we're not to go back to binocular vision and opposable thumbs—then we'll need some test for distinguishing exceptional from general causation. Roberts suggests that we do this by seeking a "point of no return": the moment at which an equilibrium that once existed ceased to do so as a result of whatever it is we're trying to explain.

The "point of no return" for the English Civil War, Roberts argues, was the imposition of a new service book on the Scottish Church in 1637.[21] Most historians would cite the American oil embargo of August 1941 as the equivalent point for the war in the Pacific.[22] But the Scottish service book would not have been introduced had there not been a Protestant Reformation and all that flowed from it; nor could Japanese aggression have occurred had Japan not modernized as a consequence of the Meiji Restoration. So the dependency of the exceptional upon the general applies in all of these cases, as does the interdependency of variables. It's our first causal test—the principle of diminishing relevance—that gives us license to emphasize some of these over others.

What we're looking for, then, as we trace processes that led to particular structures, is the point at which these processes took a distinctive, or abnormal, or unforeseen course. We're searching for phase transitions, for punctuations in some existing equilibrium, for an exceptional event that reflected general conditions but that could not have been predicted from them.[23] Or, as Aristotle put it in the *Poetics*, for those moments "when things come about contrary to expectation but because of one another."[24] How, though, do we know what the expectations prior to the event may have been?

IV.

It's here that a third procedure for establishing causation comes into play, which is the role of *counterfactuals*. Bloch argued that we should seek "the antecedent which could have been most easily avoided." We do that, he explained, by a "bold exercise of the mind" in which historians transport themselves "to the time before the event itself, in order to gauge its chances, as they appeared upon the eve of its realization." We move the present back into the past so that it becomes, as he put it, "a future of bygone times."[25]

What Bloch was suggesting here, I believe, was nothing less than the historical equivalent of laboratory experimentation in the physical sciences: using their imagination, historians were to perform procedures similar to what chemists and physicists do with their test tubes, centrifuges, and cloud chambers. They would revisit the past, varying conditions as they did so to try to see which would produce different results. They would do this by means of counterfactuals.

Now, I tried to be careful, in a previous chapter, to distinguish between laboratory and non-laboratory science. I made the point that historians can never *actually* rerun history, any more than astronomers, geologists, paleontologists, and evolutionary biologists can rerun time. But I also emphasized that these non-laboratory scientists do such experiments routinely *in their minds*. Their imaginations are their laboratories. So it is as well, Bloch was arguing, with historians. That's where counterfactuals come in: to borrow a term from Niall Ferguson, they're the historian's virtual equivalent of laboratory experimentation.[26]

E. H. Carr would not have been happy with this, and his reasons are revealing. While acknowledging that nothing is inevitable, he wondered how "can one discover a coherent sequence of cause and effect, how we can find any meaning in history, when our sequence is liable to be broken or deflected at any moment by some other, and from our point of view irrelevant, sequence?" Counterfactual history, he claimed, was just wishful thinking, especially on the part of those— like the opponents of the Bolshevik Revolution—who wished that things had come out differently.[27]

But this is yet another example of Carr confusing a particular cause with a general problem in historical causation. For if the "meaning" of history requires establishing coherent sequences of cause and effect, on the one hand, and yet nothing is inevitable, on the other hand, then it's hard to see how coherence can emerge other than from some consideration of paths not taken and an explanation of why they weren't. History is either predetermined or it isn't; and if it isn't then surely some parts of it could have happened in some other way.

Counterfactual reasoning does have to proceed, to be sure, by certain rules. You wouldn't, in a chemistry laboratory, attempt to identify a critical compound by throwing everything available—eye of newt, say, or toe of frog—into a giant bubbling cauldron to see what happens. You'd instead change only a single variable at a time while keeping the others constant. It's much the same with counterfactual history.[28]

To return to our Pearl Harbor example, it's perfectly appropriate to ask what might have happened had the United States not imposed the oil embargo on Japan after the takeover of French Indochina. It's not appropriate to ask what might have happened if the Roosevelt administration had combined that decision with an offer to transport Free French forces to that part of the world, together with a massive buildup of American forces in the Philippines, together with an effort to settle the Soviet Union's war with Nazi Germany so that Stalin could shift his forces east and also intimidate the Japanese. These were all initiatives the United States government could have attempted at the time; but to speculate on their combined effect is to produce a historiographical witches' brew where anything goes and no particular outcome is any more probable than any other.

Nor is it appropriate to change a single variable if the action involved could not have taken place at the time. It's useless to speculate, for instance, on what difference an atomic bomb or a reconnaissance satellite might have made in 1941, because these technologies were as yet undeveloped.[29] It's equally useless to wonder what would have happened if the Japanese had suddenly all become Episcopalians, or if top officials of the Roosevelt administration had developed an abrupt affinity for karaoke. Such speculation can make for bad, and less often good, science fiction;[30] but it's not history because it fails the test of plausibility. These weren't options that would have seemed feasible to decision-makers at the time.[31]

What this suggests, then, is that the use of counterfactuals in history has got to be highly disciplined. You can't throw multiple counterfactuals into the pot, because this makes it impossible to pinpoint the effect of any one of them. You can't experiment with single variables that weren't within the range of the technology or the culture of the times. Within these limits, though, counterfactual reasoning can help to establish chains of causation: to argue that the Japanese might not have attacked Pearl Harbor *if* the American oil embargo hadn't been imposed; or to claim that the Americans might not have chosen to cut off the oil flow *if* the Japanese hadn't moved into French Indochina—these are perfectly legitimate positions for historians to take.

Historians use counterfactual reasoning all the time in establishing causation, therefore, just as they distinguish between immediate, intermediate, and distant causes, just as they separate out exceptional from general causes. This still leaves the question, though, of how historians know when they've established, once and for all, the causes of any past event.

V.

The answer is, of course, that they don't.[32] Because not all sources survive, because not everything gets recorded in the sources in the first place, because the memories of participants can be unreliable, and because even if they were reliable no participant would have witnessed all of an event from all possible angles, we can never expect to get the full story of what actually happened. Maybe Napoleon's underwear was itchy on the day of Waterloo, and the great man's discomfort distracted him from the proper management of the battle. We're not likely to know this, though, because it's not the sort of thing that would have made its way into the written records. Napoleon might have found it too embarrassing to mention, even to his batman.

But let's say, counterfactually, that he did, and that the batman wrote it down. There's always the possibility that new evidence from the past will cause historians to reassess the origins of even the most familiar and agreed-upon historical events. There's even the possibility that new perspectives in the present — the possibility, say, of subjecting some surviving fragment of the offending garment to microscopic analysis to find the remains of the offending fleas — will bring about changes in what we thought we knew.[33] And even in the absence of new answers from the past, the shifting perspectives of the present can cause us to ask new questions about it that will make it look quite different, as Leo Tolstoy complained toward the end of *War and Peace*: "every year, with each new writer, opinion as to what constitutes the welfare of humanity changes; so that what once seemed good, ten years later seems bad, and vice versa. . . . [W]e even find in history, at one and the same time, quite contradictory views as to what was good and what was bad."[34]

None of this means, though, that we lack a basis for determining causes in history: it only means that our basis is a provisional one. R. G. Collingwood has argued that every new generation must rewrite history in its own way; every new historian, not content with giving new answers to old questions, must revise the questions themselves; and—since historical thought is a river into which none can step twice—even a single historian, working at a single subject for a certain length of time, finds when he tries to reopen an old question that the question has changed.[35]

There's nothing unique about this provisionality, though, for it shows up in even the hardest of the "hard" sciences. Modern science, John Ziman writes, is *evolutionary*: it's "the heir to an unbroken lineage of knowledge-acquiring organic forms, stretching back to the beginnings of life on earth. . . . It recognizes . . . that the institution as a whole is bound to change over time."[36] Or, as Joyce Appleby, Lynn Hunt, and Margaret Jacob have put it: "Science can be historically and socially framed and still be true."[37] Historians do the best they can, therefore, but our findings are subject to revision, just as they would be in any other field of human inquiry.

Within that qualification we evaluate our findings by asking *how closely our representations fit the realities we seek to explain.* I discussed this concept of "fitting" in an earlier chapter, invoking analogies to cartography, paleontology, and—at a more mundane level—tailoring. I argued that in none of these fields would we wish a perfect representation of reality, for a one-to-one correspondence between the two could produce, respectively, the one-to-one map that Jorge Luis Borges found so useless, a voracious velociraptor that only Steven Spielberg could love, and, in the case of the tailor, a naked body.[38] It's also the case that the purposes of representation vary: a world map won't help you find your way around town, just as the dinosaur model you might build for a university museum wouldn't be right for a kindergarten classroom. I'll leave any further tailoring metaphors to your imagination: my point, quite simply, is that there are boundaries between representation and reality, and that it's always a good idea to respect them.

The narrative is the form of representation that most historians use.[39] What narratives do, I've already suggested, is to *simulate* what transpired in the past. They're reconstructions, assembled within the virtual laboratories of our minds, of the processes that produced whatever structure it is we're seeking to explain. They vary in their purposes, but not in their methods. For in all of them, we ask ourselves: "How could this have happened?" We then proceed to try to answer the question in such a way as to achieve the closest possible fit between representation and reality.[40] Achieving that, however, requires several additional procedures:

First, *a preference for parsimony in consequences, but not causes*. By this, I mean that the causes we identify must converge upon a particular consequence. To return to our Pearl Harbor example, it would be quite logical to show how Japan's militarism, oil dependency, and technological prowess combined with the exposed position of the United States in the Pacific, its increasingly tough economic sanctions, and a failure of diplomacy to bring about the attack. It would be quite illogical to conclude that the attack itself then determined the course of the war, its outcome, and the nature of the postwar Japanese–American relationship. In seeking parsimony with respect to consequences, historians differ from those social scientists who value it in specifying causes. Social scientists consider an "overdetermined" event—that is, one with multiple causes—to be an inadequately explained event.[41] They do so, though, because their goal is not just to explain the past but to forecast the future. The oversimplification of causes, thus, is a necessity to them. It isn't to historians, for whom multiple causation is the only feasible basis for explanation, which is in turn—most of the time at least—the only thing they think it feasible to try to do.

Second, *the subordination of generalization to narration*. A simulation is not a system. It's a representation of what happened, but it tells us little about what's going to happen. That's why historians can qualify each detail with yet another detail, down to and beyond the level of Napoleon's fleas. This isn't to say, though, that historians don't generalize: we do this all the time, but we do it by incorporating our generalizations into our narratives rather than the other way around. There are a potentially infinite number of links in any causal chain: where did each flea come from, for example, and how did he or she attach himself or herself to the emperor's underwear, and then to the emperor? How did each of the Japanese pilots learn to fly? How did the engines in each of their planes work? What kind of underwear were *they* wearing on *their* big day? There are some things we can't know, there are some things we don't need to know, and fortunately these categories overlap to a considerable degree. We use micro-generalizations to bridge such gaps in the evidence and to move the narrative forward: they make it possible to represent reality. We resist the macro-generalizations that, by oversimplifying causes, subvert narrative, and therefore detach representation from reality. Or, to put it in terms I used in a previous chapter, we practice *particular generalization*, not *general particularization*.

Third, *a distinction between timeless and time-bound logic*. Some historical findings require no research, just common sense. You don't have to be a professional historian to understand that causes must precede consequences, or that correlations are not necessarily causes. These are universally valid propositions, at least throughout this universe.[42] What does require research is common sense uncommonly held because of distances from us in time, space, or culture. History is full of examples, as Marc Bloch insisted, of "states of mind which were formerly common, yet which appear peculiar to us because we no longer share them." It's always dangerous to exalt "to the level of the eternal observations necessarily borrowed from our own brief moment in time."[43] Sorting out the difference between how things happen and how things happened involves more than just changing a verb tense. It's an important part of what's involved in achieving that closer fit between representation and reality.

Fourth, *an integration of induction and deduction.* Since we're historians, not novelists, we're obliged to tie our narrative as closely as possible to the evidence that has survived: that's an inductive process. But we have no way of knowing, until we begin looking for evidence with the purposes of our narrative in mind, how much of it's going to be relevant: that's a deductive calculation. Composing the narrative will then produce places where more research is needed, and we're back to induction again. But that new evidence will still have to fit within the modified narrative, so we're back to deduction. And so on until, as I earlier quoted William H. McNeill, "it feels right, and then I write it up and ship it off to the publisher."[44] That's why the distinction between induction and deduction is largely meaningless for the historian seeking to establish causation. The verb "to fit," which implies both procedures, is much better. It's not just tailors who look at what they have to cover, and then at what they have with which to cover it, and then back and forth, again and again, until the fit is as good as it's going to get.

Finally, *replicability.* The representation—or narrative, or simulation—must command a consensus among those who use it that its correspondence with reality is a close one. This need not extend to every detail: where the evidence is ambiguous there's always room for disagreement among historians, just as there is among paleontologists who can't agree on the appropriate skin color for their dinosaur models, or on the likelihood of feathers. But where the evidence is *not* ambiguous and still the findings cannot be replicated—if the sources don't hold up, that is, or the logic is faulty—then a consensus is not achieved.[45] There's no absolute standard for reaching a consensus in history, or science, or even law. But there are standards that approach the absolute, nonetheless. They derive from the precedents established through repeated efforts to apply representations to realities, and through the agreements these generate on where a close fit is and is not achieved.[46]

VI.

I want to conclude with one more point about causation, contingency, and the difficulties of dealing with them: it's a plea for methodological tolerance. I once had an article turned down by a major international relations journal on the grounds that I'd indulged in paradigm pluralism. "Not allowed," the reader's report read. "You can only have one paradigm at a time."

After brooding about this for a long time, I've concluded—hardly surprisingly—that that's a short-sighted view. I'd cite, as my authority, William Whewell, who argued a century and a half ago that a situation of "rules springing from remote and unconnected quarters [but leaping] to the same point" was possible only "from *that* being the point where truth resides."[47] Well, perhaps not *only*, and perhaps not even *truth*: things looked more certain in the nineteenth century than they do now. But if you understand Whewell's argument to mean that a plurality of paradigms can converge to bring us a closer fit between representation and reality—if you accept his "leaping to the same point" as analogous to my "fitting together"—then I think you'll see the connection. It's interesting to me that scientists like Stephen Jay Gould and Edward O. Wilson have rediscovered Whewell.[48] I wonder if historians should not also do so.

For this, it seems to me, is yet another area in which history is closer to the natural sciences than to the social sciences. Historians are—or ought to be—open to diverse ways of organizing knowledge: our reliance on micro- rather than macro-generalization opens up for us a wide range of methodological approaches. Within a single narrative we can be Rankeans, or Marxists, or Freudians, or Weberians, or even postmodernists, to the extent that these modes of representation bring us closer to the realities for which we're trying to account. We're free to describe, evoke, quantify, qualify, and even reify if these techniques serve to improve the "fit" we're trying to achieve. Whatever works, in short, we should use.

Of course it's pragmatic, inconsistent, and often just plain messy. But it is, I believe, good science, for what we can learn should always figure more prominently in our set of priorities than the purity of the methods by which we learn it.

Chapter Seven

MOLECULES WITH MINDS OF THEIR OWN

THERE IS, HOWEVER, one obvious objection to my argument that at least some of the methods of the natural sciences, as currently practiced, come closer to those of historians than do those of most social scientists. It is that the so-called "hard" sciences don't deal with self-reflective, feedback-generating, information-exchanging entities, by which I mean *people*.

The issue here isn't that of consciousness, which exists in gorillas, giraffes, and presumably gerbils, even if not, as far as we know, in geraniums. What doesn't appear within any of these species, though—allowing for as yet unproven assertions about chimpanzees who calculate, or gray parrots who contemplate—is the awareness of self: the capacity to think as an individual about one's own situation, to determine a distinctive response, and to communicate it to others.[1]

The behavior of animals reflects the circumstances in which they find themselves; but this reflexivity tends not to differ much from individual to individual. It is in the aggregate, therefore, fairly predictable. Schools of fish, flocks of birds, and herds of deer respond similarly, collectively, and almost instantly to predators.[2] They don't stand (or fly or swim) around debating the matter. Human behavior is far more complicated, because the capacity for self-reflection opens the prospect of responding to similar circumstances in very dissimilar ways. No instantaneous consensus is likely. Forecasting outcomes, therefore, is at best difficult, often impossible.

The social sciences, of course, were devised to deal with these complications. They've too frequently done so, though, by attempting to impose on people the predictability that comes from studying schools of fish, flocks of birds, and herds of deer.[3] An increasingly favored mechanism these days is rational choice theory: a curious procedure that generalizes about collective human behavior by assuming *both* the rationality and the autonomy of "utility maximizing" decision makers. The possibility that "utilities" might differ among individuals, communities, institutions, nations and cultures, or that methods of "maximizing" might not thus be the same, or that feedback might occur so that each utility maximizer could affect the way in which the next one maximizes utility—these complexities do not seem much to concern the rational choice theorists. Nor is there agreement among them as to what "rationality" actually means.[4]

So is rational choice theory yet another quest for the independent variable? Its roots in economics—arguably the most reductionist of the social sciences—suggest strongly that it is. Like that discipline, it reduces complexity to simplicity in an effort to forecast the future. It seeks out equilibria, for as the Yale political scientists Donald Green and Ian Shapiro have pointed out, "unless equilibria can be discovered, lawlike statements—from which predictive hypotheses are derived—cannot be developed."[5] It is, thus, Newtonian in its assumptions about the scientific method: twentieth-century achievements in the natural sciences have made little impression on it. Neither—hardly surprisingly—has history.

Rational choice theorists fail in particular to take into account the possibility that the actions of a single individual can, under certain circumstances, *shift standards of rationality*, and hence appropriate behavior, for millions of others. They've no way of accounting, say, for

Buddha, Christ, and Mohammed, or for Alexander, Napoleon, and Hitler, or for Lincoln, Churchill, and Margaret Thatcher. Indeed it's this inability to deal with distinctive individuals—what an earlier generation, including Mrs. Thatcher, would have called "great men"— that most often causes historians to dismiss not just rational choice theory but the social sciences generally as irrelevant, sometimes the very notion of science itself.[6]

That latter conclusion may be premature, though, even within so idiosyncratic a realm as biography. There is, to be sure, a clear line separating the *objects of inquiry* in the natural sciences, on the one hand, and in the social sciences and history, on the other: the latter deal with people and the former don't. The line isn't so clear, though, when it comes to *methods of inquiry*. For here the "new" sciences of chaos and complexity, with their vivid imagery and accessible vocabulary—a vocabulary more accessible, indeed, than what one finds in most of the social sciences—may give us, metaphorically at least, new ways to account for the peculiarities of human behavior: for molecules, as it were, with minds of their own. Historians, at a minimum, should explore this possibility, and that's what I'll try to do here.

I.

One of the quirkier movies of recent years was Spike Jonze's *Being John Malkovich*. The plot features an entrepreneur who improbably gains and then sells access to the actor's mind, so that he and his customers are able to see and feel whatever Malkovich does. Critics interpreted the film as a parody of postmodernism, but it struck me— perhaps because I'm preparing one—as a commentary on biography, especially the odd combination of self-importance and self-effacement that this form of historical writing involves.

A biographer has got to see things through another person's perceptions—to take over another mind, so to speak. You've got to subdue your own distinctiveness in order to do this; otherwise your biography will reflect what's inside your own head rather than that of your subject. But sooner or later you've also got to detach yourself and regain your own identity; otherwise the biography will lack analytical depth or comparative perspective. For the characters in the movie, this meant sliding into a wormhole that dumped them out alongside the New Jersey Turnpike when their time inside Malkovich's mind had expired. For the biographer, it means resisting seduction by your subject so that you can reach your own conclusions. Either way, hard landings are to be expected.

The problem is that in the real world, as opposed to the cinematic one, the mind of another person is at least as inaccessible as the landscape of the past, even if that person is alive and in a physical sense wholly accessible.[7] Freud would insist, indeed, that portions of our minds are inaccessible even to ourselves, except through the arduous excavations of psychoanalysis. So how can biographers claim to know what went on in the minds of distant and long-dead individuals? How, as Spike Jonze might put it, do they "become" Julius Caesar, or Catherine the Great, or Vladimir Ilyich Lenin, or for that matter even John Lennon?

Part of the answer, of course, has to do with what makes the writing of any kind of history possible: past processes have generated surviving structures—documents, images, memories—that allow us to reconstruct in our minds, and then on our word processors, what happened. Like other historians, biographers fit representations to realities, but in a particular kind of way. It's not enough simply to chronicle what a person did. Biographers must also try to determine why he or she did it, and that requires retrieving a set of mental processes of which even the subject of the biography may not have been fully aware. It's this need to bridge the gap between actions, consciousness, and subconsciousness that makes biography such a daunting enterprise. It ought also to make biographers humble.

Biographers proceed, in some ways, as paleontologists do: we reconstruct as much flesh as we can from such fossils as we have. But the differences outweigh the similarities. The megalosaurus you see modeled in a museum, for example, is a static representation. Biographers can't content themselves with this, because biography must not only flesh out bones but animate them. It's like time-lapse photography: our sources are our snapshots; but the sequence in which we arrange them and the significance we attach to the gaps between them are as important as what any one of them shows. We rerun whole lives, not single moments in them.

Another difference is that biographers, unlike paleontologists, document particularity. A reconstructed animal is usually meant to represent an entire species. A reconstructed life is meant, most of the time, to represent that single life and no other.[8] We'd rarely say, as a paleontologist would almost always say, that by exhibiting a single individual we're portraying an entire class. In contrast to what happens, not just in paleontology but in any of the "hard" sciences, then, the biographer's basic subject—that is, the object to be explained—is necessarily singular.

To be sure, we can and should draw upon what the social sciences—particularly psychology and sociology—have taught us about human behavior in the aggregate, just as a paleontologist would depend heavily upon what's known about the environment in some distant age. But the aggregate is only a starting point for biography, because that discipline so determinedly resists, indeed subverts, generalization. To impose some predetermined framework on distinctive individuals—as for example Erik Erikson was accused of doing with Luther and Gandhi—smacks too much of stuffing people into glass cases. It uses the individual to exhibit a class.[9]

It follows from this that biography, like the larger sphere of history within which it resides, is at once a deductive and an inductive exercise. Patterns of human behavior extending across time and space can alert us to the kinds of questions we should be asking about the particular individual we're dealing with: that's where deduction comes in.

But these patterns alone can't determine the answers, for it's all too easy to find what you're looking for when you've already decided ahead of time what it is. The evidence of particular experience, in biography, has got to discipline what we know from collective experience: induction is how we do that.

The first stage in meeting the Malkovich test, then, is to balance the general against the particular in a far more precise way than the writing of most history demands. For induction, in biography, comes chiefly from surviving structures that a single person has left behind. Deduction draws on everything else in the human experience that might help us to understand that person. Biography demands both procedures, but in a peculiarly delicate balance. It's a little like riding a unicycle: you need to be aware all the time of a wider horizon, even as you concentrate on the single problematic point at which the rubber meets the road.

II.

A central problem for biographers is that notoriously subjective quality we call *character*. I'd define that term as a set of patterns within an individual's behavior that extend throughout his or her life. It's what causes a person to deal with dissimilar circumstances in similar ways. Even where that doesn't happen—where behavior is ambivalent or contradictory—biographers will often see consistency in the persistence of the contradictions.

We've had no very good explanation, though, of how we recognize character when we see it. People's lives are full of patterns. Which are the particular ones that constitute character? To answer this question, think for a moment about how biographers work. They generally begin at the micro-level, with birth, childhood, and adolescence, because they assume that that's where character is formed. They proceed, then, to the macro-level as they chronicle whatever it was as an adult that made the subject of the biography worth writing about. Biography, like life, is a matter of expanding horizons and then usually, as old age sets in, contracting them once again. And biographers tend to regard as character those elements of personality that remain constant, or nearly so, throughout.

What is this procedure, though, if not something we've already encountered from chaos and complexity theory: a search for self-similarity across scale? The scale, in this instance, is the widening and then narrowing sphere of a person's life. Like practitioners of fractal geometry, biographers seek patterns that persist as one moves from micro- to macro-levels of analysis, and back again. "[T]he most outstanding exploits do not always . . . [reveal] the goodness or badness of the agent," Plutarch wrote nearly two thousand years ago: "often, in fact, a casual action, the odd phrase, or a jest reveals character better than battles involving the loss of thousands upon thousands of lives, huge troop movements, and whole cities besieged."[10]

It follows from this that the scale across which we seek similarity need not be chronological. Consider the following incidents in the life of Stalin between 1929 and 1940, arranged not by dates but in terms of ascending horror. Start with the parrot he kept in a cage in his Kremlin apartment. The dictator had the habit of pacing up and down for long periods of time, smoking his pipe, brooding, and occasionally spitting on the floor. One day the parrot tried to mimic Stalin's spitting. He immediately reached into the cage with his pipe and crushed the parrot's head. A very micro-level event, you might well say, so what?

But then you learn that Stalin, while on vacation in the Crimea, was once kept awake by a barking dog. It turned out to be a seeing-eye dog that belonged to a blind peasant. The dog wound up being shot, and the peasant wound up in the Gulag. And then you learn that Stalin drove his independently minded second wife, who tried to talk back to him, into committing suicide. And that he arranged for Trotsky, who also talked back, to be assassinated halfway around the world. And that he arranged as well the deaths of as many of Trotsky's associates as he could reach, as well as the deaths of hundreds of thousands of other people who never had anything to do with Trotsky. And that when his own people began to talk back by resisting the collectivization of agriculture, he allowed some fourteen million of them to die from the resulting starvation, exile, or imprisonment.[11]

Again there's self-similarity across scale, except that the scale this time is a body count. It's a fractal geometry of terror. Stalin's character extended across time and space, to be sure, but what's most striking about it is its extension across scale: the fact that his behavior seemed much the same in large matters, small matters, and most of those that lay in between. "[A] painter reproduces his subject's likeness by concentrating on the face and the expression of the eyes," Plutarch adds, "by means of which character is revealed."[12] A biographer must be similarly sensitive.

Do fractals then give us a scientific basis for characterizing character? I wouldn't want to push the argument that far. Our "measurements" of this quality will never be as precise, or as replicable, as the ones scientists can now make of drainage patterns, mountain slopes, blood vessels, stalks of cauliflower, and of course the British coastline. What fractals do suggest, though, is something we don't often hear about biography: that it transcends the familiar dimensions of time and space to deal with scale as well.

In one way, we've known this all along. When we speak of "fleshing out" our portrayal of some historical figure, we surely mean this in more than a two-dimensional sense. But what, exactly, has been that third dimension: the additional step, beyond simply tracing an individual's time and place in the past, toward getting inside someone else's mind? Biographers—and critics of biography—have been very vague about this: we knew what we were talking about, but until recently we didn't have the vocabulary for it, or the means of visualizing it. Character may be an unscientific concept within the framework of the old physical, biological, and social sciences. Within the framework of the new I'm not so sure, anymore, that it is.

III.

What is it, though, that brings distinctive characters in history to the attention of the historian in the first place? It is of course *reputation*, or, to put it another way, some surviving structure that causes us to assign some special significance to the processes that produced it. The establishment of a dynasty, the discovery of a continent, the founding of a religion, the conquest of a country, the creation of a work of art, the destruction—or attempted destruction—of an entire people: all of these are processes that have become significant to us because their results survive and shape our consciousness, whether as faiths, institutions, technologies, poems, plays, paintings, novels, symphonies, memories, or ghosts.

These standards of significance, however, can shift, for reasons that have much to do with the instruments we use to measure, or map, the past.[13] It was always going to be the case that Hitler would meet our test of significance: that was clear even in his lifetime, and certainly to himself.[14] But what about Victor Klemperer, a quiet Dresden philologist of whom few people had heard until just a few years ago? What brought Klemperer to our attention—to such an extent that the history of the Third Reich today can hardly be written without him—was a set of improbable circumstances: he was a Jew, he kept a very thorough diary, and he survived.[15]

History is full of people who seemed unimportant to their contemporaries but, through some process that produced a surviving structure, have become important to us. There are far more references in Liza Picard's history of Restoration London to Samuel Pepys, for example, than to Charles II: as in the case of Klemperer, the critical difference was a diary.[16] No one would have expected that an Amherst, Massachusetts, recluse would become, arguably, the most influential American poet of the nineteenth century, but what Emily Dickinson left behind, after being called back, made her so. And of course it was the failure of his target to survive—the fact that the structures left behind were a shattered skull and a legacy—that established an ineradicable place in history for a young Texas misfit who happened to bring a rifle to work along with his lunch one morning in Dallas in November 1963.

Historians have rarely tried to specify, though, whatever it is that causes certain individuals to stand out from all the rest. Most people go through life, after all, without it ever occurring to them, or to anyone else, that their biographies would be worth writing. Something happens in some situations to change that, but the unpredictabilities involved in the process have discouraged efforts to generalize about it. We usually just chalk it up to chance or—for the more portentous among us—destiny.

If the idea of self-similarity across scale can sharpen our definitions of character, though, why shouldn't another concept from the new sciences—that of sensitive dependence on initial conditions— help us out with historical distinctiveness? I'd venture the hypothesis that in every instance in which historians have singled out one individual from masses of others, it's because there's been a moment of sensitivity: some point at which small shifts at the beginning of a process produced large consequences at the end of it.

I don't mean to suggest that this works with big events for which there are multiple interacting causes. When it comes to issues like the rise and fall of empires, overdetermination builds in a redundancy that makes it difficult to specify initial conditions: these are constantly occurring, recurring, and overlapping one another, which is why it's unlikely that Cleopatra's nose caused the fall of Egypt or Rome, whatever else it may have caused the rise of.

Sensitive dependence may, though, determine the emergence of distinctive individuals in history. We often refer to it, imprecisely, as a matter of being in the right place at the right time—something Cleopatra certainly did manage to do. But it could also involve leaving the right things behind, an important prerequisite for biography. For even the lives of ordinary people could hardly be written had not some extraordinary source had the extraordinary luck to survive. The production and preservation of a particular archive, therefore, could be as significant an event as the sinking of a particular dinosaur into a particular bog somewhere that nonetheless tells us much of what we know about the general conditions of life in an otherwise inaccessible era.

But what is it—apart from leaving an extraordinary source behind—that causes us to regard someone as worthy of a biography? What do we really mean by being in the right place at the right time? It's not just the overcoming of obstacles, for plenty of prominent figures in the past have had their way paved for them. It's not the inheritance of status or wealth either, for lots of people acquire both in history without acquiring biographies. Historians have wrestled for a long time with the prerequisites for conspicuousness, but maybe they've been going at it in the wrong way.

Perhaps they should think more about the circumstances in which reputation emerges. For if I'm right about sensitive dependence, it's a moment at which there's sufficient underdetermination that the actions of an individual can make a difference. Some such circumstances are always with us: assassinations, for example, can take place at any time; and although some, like the unsuccessful attempt on Hitler's life, have purposes behind them that might have made them predictable, others, like the successful attack on Kennedy, do not, leaving us with a tragedy all the more traumatic for its absence of evident purpose.

Most of the time, though, the circumstances that make individuals conspicuous—that allow reputations to emerge—have to do with the existence of what we might call windows of opportunity. The industrial revolution created an opening for someone—it happened to be Karl Marx—to characterize and then condemn the workings of capitalism in a sufficiently plausible way as to gain a mass following, something that probably wouldn't have happened had Marx been writing fifty years earlier or later. Great war leaders like Pericles or the Pitts might hardly have been noticed had it not been for the conflicts during which they came to power. How many potential Napoleons have there been of whom we've never heard because they sought ascendancy but lacked the opportunities that could bring it about? How many Osama bin Ladens?[17]

I suggested earlier that sensitive dependence in science almost always results from a phase transition: a point at which the properties of a substance are shifting to something else. Is this what we mean by windows of opportunity in history? Might we be able to draw upon the language of science to sharpen our thinking about what produced points of sensitive dependence in the past? Maybe—but almost certainly not with respect to the future. For while scientists can say something in general terms about the properties of phase transitions, they can rarely predict the precise course the events that occur within them are going to take.[18] They can only recover those in retrospect. That's about the best we can expect to do in history as well.

IV.

There is one other thing, though, that biographers—and historians generally—can't escape doing that natural scientists never have to do: it's to make moral judgments. Nobody worries, within the "hard" sciences, about the morality of molecules. Even quarks, whatever their assigned properties of color, flavor, and charm, have yet to be regarded as good or evil. But no work of history of which I'm aware has ever been written without making some kind of statement—explicitly or implicitly, consciously or subconsciously—about where its subjects lie along the ubiquitous spectrum that separates the admirable from the abhorrent. You can't escape thinking about history in moral terms. Nor, I believe, should you try to do so.

The reason is that we are, unlike all others, moral animals. No society operates without some sense of what's right and wrong: even Hitler knew that the Holocaust was immoral, or he wouldn't have gone to the efforts he did to try to conceal it.[19] To try to purge human behavior of a moral sense is to deny what distinguishes it. You'd be writing the histories of schools of fish, flocks of birds, and herds of deer, not people.

The issue for historians, then, is not whether we should make moral judgments, but how we can do so responsibly, by which I mean in such a way as to convince both the professionals and non-professionals who'll read our work that what we say makes sense. That's tougher now than it used to be, given the postmodernist insight — accurate in my opinion — that all of our bases for evaluating behavior are themselves artifacts of behavior. We used to have firm foundations upon which to stand. We have them no longer.[20]

It doesn't follow from this, though, that because our findings inescapably reflect who we are and where we've been, no one of them is any more valid than any other. To make this case, I'd like to return once again to the *methods* of the natural sciences, despite the fact that the *objects* of our inquiry are clearly not the same.

A good place to start is a place we've visited several times before: the British coastline. Remember that, as Lewis Richardson and Benoit Mandelbrot have reminded us, there's no way of knowing its actual length: the answer varies as our units of measurement do. At the same time, though, I argued earlier that we'd be most unwise to conclude from this, as a postmodernist might, that Britain is not actually there: that we might safely sail a supertanker — let us call it the *Paul de Man* perhaps, or the *Jacques Derrida* — right through it.

I use this example to underscore a point I've tried to make several times: that we must accord *equal* status, as historians, to representation, on the one hand, and to reality, on the other. To deny representation is to deprive ourselves of all the information our own eyes and ears can't gather. Our postmodernist vessel would be operating without maps, compasses, computers, radios, or radar. To deny reality, though, is to detach representation from whatever's being represented: you allow the absence of definitive conclusions from your instruments to convince you that there's nothing at all out there. Either way, you're apt to wind up on the rocks.

This is where the Malkovich maneuver becomes critical for a biographer. Your subject's mind—the one you've got to get into—is a reality you can't change. It's like the rocks and shoals that are going to be there no matter which ship is sailing toward them and no matter which unit of measurement its navigator is using in trying to detect them. There's no arguing with this reality: you've got to accept, as a biographer, who your subject was, for better or for worse. No sweeping of dirt under the rug; but no halos either.

You can't accomplish this without empathy, which is not the same thing as sympathy. Getting inside other people's minds requires that your own mind be open to their impressions—their hopes and fears, their beliefs and dreams, their sense of right and wrong, their perception of the world and where they fit within it. "History cannot be scientifically written," R. G. Collingwood insisted, "unless the historian can re-enact in his own mind the experience of the people whose actions he is narrating." [21] The resulting impressions will never be the same as your own. Some of them may enchant you; others may horrify you. Still, you've got to reconstruct them, for that's the only way you can understand the reasons your subject had for behaving as he or she did. And surely even in a biography of Caligula you'd want to allow that much autonomy. [22]

But then you bail out. You don't wait to be dumped alongside the New Jersey Turnpike, you jump for it. You carry with you, of course, a set of representations of where you've been. You've turned yourself away from the rocks, however, which means that you're free to measure the subject of your biography in any metric you like. You're depicting the reality you've vicariously experienced, and you're fully in charge as you do so: it's your own autonomy you need to worry about now. What's important is that you make these representations *only* after having acquainted yourself—by means of empathy—with the reality they characterize.

Because no two historians will ever perform this task in just the same way, there can be no single standard for objectivity in biography, or for that matter in all of history. There'll never be a consensus on the reputation of Peter the Great, any more than there'll be on the length of the British coastline. There certainly is a consensus, though, on the existence of both, and indeed on the fact that the former once sailed along the latter. So how do we bridge this gap between what we know and what we can only argue about?

We do it, I think, by coming back to the idea of "fitting" representation to reality. The judgments any historian applies to the past can't help but reflect the present the historian inhabits. These will surely shift, as present concerns do. History is constantly being remeasured in terms of previously neglected metrics: recent examples include the role of women, minorities, discourse, sexuality, disease, and culture. All of these carry moral implications, and they by no means exhaust the list. But the history these representations represent has not changed. It's back there in the past, just as solidly as that still imprecisely measured coastline. It's this reality that keeps our representations from flying off into fantasy.

The act of fitting representations to realities allows us to approximate consensus, rather in the way that, in the calculus, we approach but never quite attain the curve. Of course there'll be disagreements among historians about how to do this, but these differences are themselves among the means of approximation: think of them as the historiographical equivalent of cartographic triangulation. When the British undertook the Great Trigonometrical Survey of India in the mid-nineteenth century, they did it by just such methods: they started at the coast and wound up in the Himalayas, mapping each point in the landscape with reference to at least two others. They used divergent perspectives to impose a single grid, from which they proceeded, with great success, to represent a complex reality.[23]

Something like that, I believe, is how historians go about mapping the moral as well as the physical landscape of the past, a point I'll develop more fully in the final chapter. Suffice it to say here that there is no one "correct" metric; but that through the Malkovich maneuver— this process of getting into and back out of another person's mind, and then arguing among ourselves over what we saw there—we do manage to view the past from its own perspective as well as our own. That's what biography, but also history, is largely about.

V.

At this point, however, I must confess to having strayed quite far from the views of the two historians who inspired this book, Marc Bloch and E. H. Carr. For neither would have accepted my view that historians have no choice but to make moral judgments. Bloch was uncharacteristically vehement on the subject:

> Are we so sure of ourselves and our age as to divide the company of our forefathers into the just and the damned? . . . [S]ince nothing is more variable than such judgments, subject to all the fluctuations of collective opinion or personal caprice, history, by all too frequently preferring the compilation of honor rolls to that of notebooks, has gratuitously given itself the appearance of the most uncertain of disciplines. Hollow indictments are followed by vain rehabilitations. Robespierrists! Anti-Robespierrists! For pity's sake, simply tell us what Robespierre was.[24]

Carr was no less forthright. It was for contemporaries, not posterity, to judge the great figures of history, he insisted: indeed the "principal embarrassment" of the contemporary historian was the difficulty of resisting just this tendency. Historians had every right to condemn such institutions as despotism or slavery. They had no right, though, to pass judgment on individual slave-owners, or to denounce the individual sins of Charlemagne or Napoleon. "Stalin is said to have behaved cruelly and callously to his second wife," Carr acknowledged; "but as a historian of Soviet affairs, I do not feel myself much concerned."[25]

What's implied here, I think, is the assumption that times impose their morality upon lives: that there's no point in condemning individuals for the circumstances in which they find themselves. Perhaps that's true in most cases. But the twentieth century saw at least three horrendous examples of lives imposing their morality upon times: what Hitler did in Germany, what Lenin and Stalin did in the Soviet Union, and what Mao Zedong did in China. Neither Bloch nor Carr provides guidance as to how historians should deal with such situations.

Bloch himself became the victim of one of them. He could hardly have foreseen his own execution at the hands of the Gestapo when he was writing *The Historian's Craft*: even so, it's a remarkably tolerant book given the harrowing circumstances under which it was composed. That's part of its appeal, but it's also, sadly, an evasion, for nothing in it would explain the rise or the nature of Nazi Germany. Should historians of that period have contented themselves, as in the case of Robespierre, with simply telling us what Hitler was, and leaving it at that? Bloch never got around to saying.

Carr's reluctance to pass judgment on the Soviet Union is even more disturbing, for he had ample evidence of Stalin's crimes and yet sought to shroud them in utilitarian calculations about the price of what he called "progress." "Every great period of history has its casualties as well as its victories," he wrote in *What Is History?* "The thesis that the good of some justifies the suffering of others is implicit in all government, and is just as much a conservative as a radical doctrine."[26] Carr admitted privately that he had "rather by-passed the horrors and brutalities and persecutions. . . . But are they the things on which one ought to concentrate if one wants to get at the ultimate significance of the revolution?"[27] Maybe not, but what if the horrors, brutalities, and persecutions *were* the ultimate significance of the revolution?

History happens to historians, as well as to everyone else. The idea that the historian can or should stand aloof from moral judgments unrealistically denies that fact. It implies a detachment of observation from evaluation that's at odds with what both Bloch and Carr quite rightly said about the impossibility of objectivity in history.[28] The only way around this problem, I think, is to accept the historian's engagement with the morality of his or her time, but to distinguish that engagement explicitly—as the Malkovich procedure requires the biographer to do—from the morality of the individual, or the age, the historian is writing about. We need both angles of vision if we really are to triangulate the past.

VI.

I fear that that this chapter has staggered, even more than the others, under the weight of the metaphors I've inflicted on it: John Malkovich, the New Jersey Turnpike, Cleopatra's nose, Stalin's parrot, the British coastline, the good ship *Jacques Derrida*, the Indian Great Survey, plus the usual assortment of dinosaurs. If I'd told you at the beginning that these were the topics to be covered, you'd have anticipated a considerable amount of disarray. You may even have found it.

I make no apologies for metaphors, however, mixed or otherwise. For it seems to me that empathy—whether with respect to the past, the present, or the future—absolutely requires them. If we're to be open to impressions, which is what I've argued empathy means, we've also got to be comparative. And that, in turn, is just another way of saying that something is "like" something else. It comes with being a self-reflective, feedback-generating, information-exchanging (if not always utility-maximizing) entity.

If metaphors help us think—if, to use yet a final one, they can open windows and let in fresh air—then we have every reason to rely on them, and to do so unashamedly. We need all the help we can get.

Chapter Eight

SEEING LIKE A HISTORIAN

I BEGAN AND ENDED the first chapter in this book with two images, created 180 years apart, of backs turned toward us: Caspar David Friedrich's 1818 painting *The Wanderer above a Sea of Fog*, in which a young man standing on a promontory contemplates a landscape he knows is there but can't see; and the final scene from John Madden's 1998 film, *Shakespeare in Love*, in which Gwyneth Paltrow, as Viola at the beginning of *Twelfth Night*, wades ashore alone on a deserted beach, which, as the camera pulls back, is revealed to be an uncharted continent. I suggested that if you think of the past as a kind of landscape, then the historian is in something like the position of the two figures portrayed here: the simultaneous sense of significance and insignificance, of detachment and engagement, of mastery and humility, of adventure but also of danger. Being suspended between these polarities, I argued, is what historical consciousness is all about.

The intervening chapters have focused on how historians achieve that state: the manipulation of time, space, and scale; the derivation of past processes from surviving structures; the particularization of generalization; the integration of randomness with regularity; the differentiation of causes; the obligation to get inside the mind of another person, or another age, but then to find your way out again. Through all of this I've indulged outrageously in metaphors—everything from Marmite spilled along the M-40 to postmodernist supertankers plowing toward the British coastline—as a means of pushing you into looking at some familiar issues in unfamiliar ways, rather in the way that Gertrude Stein found herself doing when she flew across the United States in 1938 and was surprised to see the landscape below taking on the lines, shapes, and colors of cubist art.[1]

Which brings me to yet another landscape seen from above. It's on the cover of my Yale colleague James C. Scott's recent book, *Seeing Like a State*. It shows two apparently inexplicable right-angle bends in a road built across a flat North Dakota prairie. There is an explanation, though: the roads follow township boundaries laid out on the sys-

North Dakota road adjusting for the convergence
of longitude lines as they approach the North Pole. Alex S. MacLean
photograph, © 1994, reproduced in James Corner and
Alex S. MacLean, *Taking Measures across the American Landscape*
(New Haven: Yale University Press, 1996), p. 56.

tem of six-square-mile grids which the United States government imposed, not just on North Dakota but on all of the American Midwest, when it surveyed that territory during the nineteenth century. The bends in the road reflect the fact that lines of longitude converge as you move toward the North Pole; hence the boundaries and the roads following them must adjust as well.[2] Perish the thought, in this state-sanctioned method of road building, that there should be anything other than ninety-degree angles in making the adjustments. No short cuts allowed.

Now contrast this with one of the most elegant public spaces in Europe, which happens to lie in the middle of Oxford. No government designed the great curve of the High as it sweeps from Carfax down to Magdalen bridge, and no architect did either. Rather it was created by cattle: as the name of the town suggests, it was the path taken by oxen making their way from the ford across the Thames or Isis to the one across the Cherwell, and back again.[3]

Scott uses his North Dakota image to symbolize what states try to do to those portions of the earth's surface they hope to control, and to the people who live upon them. For it's only by making territories and societies *legible*—by which he means *measurable* and hence *manipulable*—that governments can impose and maintain their authority. "These state simplifications," he writes, are "like abridged maps." They don't replicate what's actually there, but "when allied with state power, [they] enable much of the reality they [depict] to be remade."[4] Not all of it, though, for there remain plenty of places like Oxford where governments had no choice but to retrofit their authority to what was already there.

The evidence of state-sought reality remaking is all around us: in the Roman roads that remain straighter than any of the others on British road maps; in the property lines that date back to William the Conqueror's *Domesday Book*; in the fact that almost all of us now have surnames, a late medieval equivalent of a national identity number; in the standardization of weights, measures, languages, time zones, and

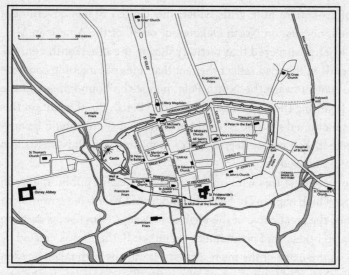

OXFORD IN 1250

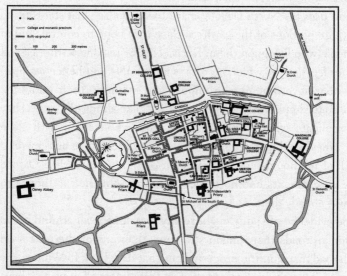

OXFORD IN 1500

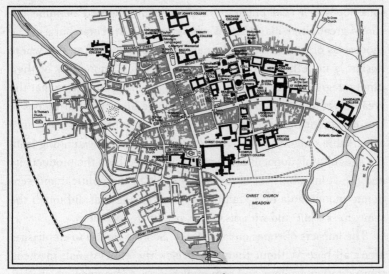

OXFORD IN 1850

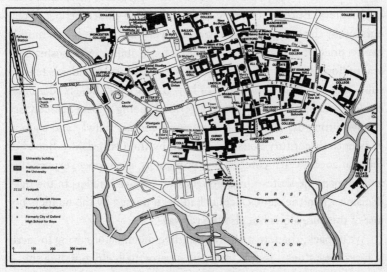

OXFORD IN 1990

Oxford's accommodation to oxen. The High in 1250, 1500, 1850,
and 1990. From John Prest, ed., *The Illustrated History of Oxford University*
(Oxford: Oxford University Press, 1993), pp. xvi–xxi.

(one hopes soon) cell phones; in the artificially imposed monumental-ism of great cities like Paris, Washington, and St. Petersburg, or the thousands of unmonumental small towns in middle America where design is nonetheless present in the relentless monotony of their ninety-degree intersections; in the straight-line boundaries that the great imperial powers projected across huge unexplored stretches of late nineteenth-century Africa; but also, as Scott points out, in a remarkable range of twentieth-century phenomena extending from the agricultural monoculture that has increased both the productivity and the vulnerability of crops and animals to the political and eco-nomic monomania of a Stalin or a Mao Zedong that did much the same, for a while and with disastrous results, for people.

The impacts of states on landscapes, Scott is careful to emphasize, aren't all bad. Without them, we'd lack the educational, medical, transportation, welfare, and communication services upon which soci-ety as we know it depends.[5] We'd not have progressed much beyond the medieval Europe of singing birds and plague-ridden people so cel-ebrated by the authors of time-travel novels. But there has definitely been a price: it is that the state's search for legibility, by imposing gen-eral uniformity, diminishes local diversity. Universal standards tend to submerge particular knowledge of how things work. One reader of an earlier version of this book has described seeing a fifteenth-century cottage sitting dry alongside a nineteenth-century railway and a group of twentieth-century houses swamped by the Oxfordshire floods of the year 2000: "What combination of memory, experience, expectation and chance," he writes, "had brought [the cottage builder] to the right decision when the same calculus had been missed by the builders not just of the bungalows but also the railway?"[6]

We're back, then, to a Heisenberg-like dilemma of having to sacri-fice certain values—in this instance, a perpetually dry building site—in order to achieve certain others: a quick smooth train ride to London, for example, or reasonably affordable houses with central heating. We make trade-offs every day between the old and the new, the particular and the general, the distinctive and the democratic. We benefit from the grid modernity imposes on our lives, even as the quiet logic of antiquity continues to surprise and impress us.

And what does all of this have to do with the landscape of history? It's simply this: the possibility that historians may stand, in their relationship to the past, in something like the position states do in their relationship to territory and society. For in "mapping" the past, the historian too is laying down a grid, stifling particularity, privileging legibility, all with a view to making the past accessible for the present and the future. As is also the case with states, the effect is both constraining and liberating: we oppress the past even as we free it.

So once again historical consciousness turns out to involve no single quality but rather a tension between opposites. This one especially raises questions about what the study of history is actually for. These are the themes I want to explore in this final chapter.

I.

Let me begin with oppression, and with one particular oppressor. It was myself as a young historian of the Cold War, writing while many of the participants in the events I was describing were still alive. They were, for the most part, proud of what they'd done and eager to know how history would regard them. They found my work, on the whole, disappointing: few of them felt that I'd fully understood the crises they'd confronted, or that I'd given adequate attention—and, let it be added, sufficient applause—to the solutions they'd devised. I frequently found myself explaining to one or another of these elder statesmen that, while I respected their recollections, I'd had to balance these against those of others, and all of this against what the archives had shown. They, in turn, acknowledged the necessity of such a procedure, but still found ways, at once plaintive and condescending, to pose the following question: "How can you know what it was really like? After all, I was there, and you I believe were five at the time."

A professional nightmare that haunts historians is that the people we write about might somehow return, like King Hamlet's ghost, to let us know what they think of what we've written. From their point of view, I don't doubt, we'd come across as oppressors, perhaps even torturers or executioners.[7] The fact that, however old we are, we'd seem to them callow youths would only add insult to the injury. I see no way around this problem for, as I've repeatedly tried to stress, history, like cartography, is necessarily a *representation* of reality. It's not reality itself; indeed, if truth be told it's a pitiful approximation of a reality that, even with the greatest skill on the part of the historian, would seem very strange to anyone who'd actually lived through it.

And yet, with the passage of time, our representations *become* reality in the sense that they compete with, insinuate themselves into, and eventually replace altogether the firsthand memories people have of the events through which they've lived. Historical knowledge submerges participants' knowledge of what took place: historians impose themselves upon the past just as effectively—but also as suffocatingly—as states do upon the territories they seek to control. We make the past legible, but in doing so we lock it up in a prison from which there's neither escape nor ransom nor appeal.

Historians do this, to be sure, without malign intent. There's no conspiracy here, because this is the way everyone manages memory. We've all had the experience of what we really remember about the past getting swallowed up in some representation of the past: an anecdote so often repeated—and embellished—that it takes on a life of its own; a photograph depicting a single moment that, by surviving, becomes all we can recall of a person, or a place, or a time; a diary entry that packages the past so self-servingly that it quickly becomes the past itself.

What's happened is that we've made the past controllable through *constructed* memories, which we very much prefer to uncontrollable and therefore embarrassing or even terrifying memories. It's a natural psychological mechanism, well understood by that greatest of all students of memory management, Sigmund Freud. The historian's method of making the past accessible isn't all that different, then, from the means by which the individual makes the past bearable: there's much that we suppress, whether consciously or unconsciously, just as there's much else that we choose, quite deliberately, to emphasize.

Winston Churchill, who so effectively combined the making and writing of history, understood this point well: "History will treat me kindly," he once quipped, "because I propose to write it." But despite the thousands of pages he did in fact produce, Churchill at the end of his career was given a painfully sharp reminder that the representations of him that would survive him might not please him. "A remarkable example of modern art," he growled when Graham Sutherland's official portrait, commissioned by Parliament, was unveiled in 1954.

Winston Churchill at his eightieth-birthday celebration, with the portrait he did not like (© Hulton-Deutsch Collection / CORBIS).

But the great man hated this portrayal of himself as a querulous old man, not as the formidable bulldog who'd faced down Hitler. No doubt he would like to have done what Clementine Churchill did in fact soon do: burn the portrait.[8]

I shudder to think how many historical figures would like to have done the same to the histories written about them—or perhaps even to the historians who wrote them. Ask yourself how many of Picasso's models would have recognized themselves in his portraits. Then put a historian in Picasso's place and, say, King Henry VIII, or Theodore Roosevelt, or Nikita Khrushchev in the position of the model. You begin to see the problem. The Churchill solution doesn't really work, though, for however much power one may have had in one's life, it ultimately must yield to the power of those who'll represent the life. It was, after all, Ernst Neizvestny, whose art Khrushchev once described as "dog shit," who wound up designing his tombstone.[9]

"Reality is not only experience, it is immediate experience," R. G. Collingwood pointed out. "But thought divides, distinguishes, mediates; therefore just so far as we think about reality, we deform it by destroying its immediacy, and thus thought can never grasp reality."[10] Or, to put it another way, thought can grasp reality only in the same way that artists grasp images, states grasp landscapes, and historians grasp history: by destroying its immediacy, by dividing it, distinguishing it, mediating it, in short by representing it. To reconstruct the real past is to construct an accessible but deformed past: it is to oppress the past, to constrain its spontaneity, to deny its liberty.

II.

That's the dark side, but fortunately it's not the only side. For the historian who oppresses the past is also at the same time liberating the past, in much the same way that states, however much they may impose themselves on landscapes, still make it possible for most of us to live comfortably within them most of the time. Only the most extreme anarchist would want to eliminate the state and its infrastructure altogether. It's much the same with the writing of history. If it promised no benefits at all, then why would those who make history be as interested as they are in what those who compose it—whether they're grizzled dons or peach-fuzzed undergraduates—are going to say about them?

From the earliest orally transmitted epics through the most recent presidential library fund-raising campaign, there's always been the belief on the part of those who do great deeds that their reputations should somehow survive them. The process has always required a *commemorator*, whether it's a blind poet reciting verses around an ancient Greek campfire or the most contemporary, well-connected, and well-compensated biographer. Whoever they are, they preserve the past by making it legible and hence retrievable. And hope springs eternal among the makers of history that these recorders of history will treat them favorably. Even Hitler, in his bunker, was certain that history would vindicate him.[11]

He was right about that in at least one sense, which is that historians do liberate their subjects from the prospect of being forgotten. Most of us understand that the physical remains we'll leave behind will be unimpressive: a few bones or a pile of ashes, for example, or maybe if we're particularly notorious a shrunken head like that of Oliver Cromwell, which is said to have bounced around Cambridge for several centuries before being quietly interred, supposedly in the master's garden at Sydney Sussex.[12] We hope for more dignified forms of commemoration: a tombstone, a memorial plaque, a named building or professorship if we can afford it, or perhaps if we can't at least a portrait in a college dining hall gazing down on students who are sure to be more interested in the food (and in each other) than in who's hanging on the wall. Historians perform that commemorative function for the great but dead: for however much we may imprison them within a particular representation, we do at least free them from oblivion.[13]

To the extent that we place our subjects in context, we also rescue the world that surrounded them. As I tried to point out in an earlier chapter, historians surpass even science fiction writers in their ability, through the manipulation of time, space, and scale, to recover lost worlds.[14] We portray societies that may—like the Romans—or may not—like so many peasant cultures—have left their own monuments behind. We liberate the ones that have from their self-proclaimed grandiosity: we try not to confuse how they wanted to be seen with who they actually were. And we try to free those who left no monuments from the resulting silences, whether imposed upon them by others, or by themselves.[15] Either way, in an almost Proustian sense, we breathe life into whatever remains from another time, and we thereby assure it a kind of permanence.

It follows that we should also free the people and the societies we write about from tyrannies of judgment imported from other times and places. If it's hard for a man to cross a mountain because he thinks there might be devils lurking there, Collingwood once wrote, then "it is folly for the historian, preaching at him across a gulf of centuries, to say 'This is sheer superstition. There are no devils at all. Face the facts.'"[16] Historians must not confuse the passage of time with the accumulation of intelligence by assuming that we're smarter now than they were then. We may have more information or better technology or easier methods of communication, but this doesn't necessarily mean that we're any more skillful at playing the cards we've been dealt. Good historians take the past on its own terms first, and only then impose their own. They guard against what Stephen Jay Gould has called the greatest of all historical errors: "arrogantly judging our forebears in the light of modern knowledge perforce unavailable to them."[17]

This, in turn, means freeing not just the great but also the obscure in history from determinism: from the conviction that things could only have happened in the way that they did. Gould, who understood history better than most historians, is emphatic on this point: "the essence of history . . . is contingency," he insists, "and contingency is a thing unto itself, not the titration of determinism by randomness."[18] History is determined only *as it happens*. Nothing, apart from the passage of time itself, is inevitable. There are always choices, however unpromising these may have seemed at the time. Our responsibility as historians is as much to show that there were paths *not* taken as it is to explain the ones that were, and that too I think is an act of liberation.

Finally, when historians contest interpretations of the past among themselves, they're liberating it in yet another sense: from the possibility that there can be only a single valid explanation of what happened. It's easy to feel yourself the victim of oppression or worse when your book comes out and your fellow historians trash it in the reviews. We ought to console ourselves, though, with the thought that by debating alternative perspectives on the past, we're allowing it breathing room. We're showing that the meaning of history isn't fixed when the making of history—and even the writing of history—is finished. That's liberation as well.

I can conceive of another kind of ghost, therefore, that could haunt historians as well as everyone else if these liberations of the past aren't performed: it's our own haunted spirits, locked up within a prison that's a future in which no one respects or perhaps even remembers us. That would be at least as painful an incarceration as the one living historians impose upon ghosts from the past; and it's why we should allow that such ghosts, fearing the alternative of oblivion, might welcome being locked up in a prison of representation.

III.

But patterns of oppression and liberation in history don't just flow from what historians do to those who made it. For the past weighs so heavily upon the present and the future that these last two domains of time hardly have meaning apart from it. Whether they take the form of the language in which we think and speak, the institutions within which we function, the culture within which we exist, or even the physical landscape within which we move, the constraints history has imposed perfuse our lives, just as oxygen does our bodies.

They're particularly evident in a place like Oxford, where accretions from the past so often impede straightforward progress from pub to pub, or from book to reader in the library system, or from outdated to updated curricula. "So why did you come?" I asked one student who was complaining about these inefficiencies. "Oh, because it's so charming," he instantly replied. It is indeed, and one of the reasons, I think, is that the burden of history rests relatively comfortably there. Like the High and the many forms of traffic that have flowed down it over the centuries, Oxford's people and its past have evolved together. They've not always done so harmoniously, to be sure; but things never reached the point at which the people felt it necessary totally to uproot the past. They were thus spared the consequence that so often follows from such experiments, which is that the past then turns upon and uproots the people.

By uprooting the past, I mean what happens when someone seeks to marginalize or even eliminate something he or she doesn't like in the present by rewriting history in such a way as to accomplish that end. It can take the form of forgeries like the *Protocols of the Elders of Zion*, that fake document that led to so much real misery for Jews in the nineteenth and twentieth centuries. It can result from imagining a community, the process that is the basis for most nationalism, which implies the exclusion or persecution of those not part of the community.[19] It can involve discovering a direction in which history is moving, as Marx did, thereby providing Lenin and his followers with a justification for suppressing all classes other than "proletarians." It can surely show up as discrimination, whether on the basis of gender, race, ethnicity, sexuality, disability, or simply appearance, all of which require constructing some historical sense that certain people are superior to others. It can even take the form of deconstruction as practiced by some postmodernists, who confuse the indisputable fact that social constructions do exist with the highly disputable proposition that their own findings are not among them.

In each of these instances history is enlisted in some act of oppression: the past is reconstructed — which is to say that it's made *legible* in some particular way—with a view to constraining someone else's freedom in the future. Historians too often have participated in this process, but it's hardly confined to them. The search for a past with which to attempt to control the future is inseparable from human nature: it's what we mean when we say we learn from experience. What's frightening about this process is when it targets victims: when excuses for marginalization lead to discrimination and then to the next logical step, which is authoritarianism. I'd go so far as to define that term as what occurs when a reconstructed past produces the belief, in the mind of some leader in the present, that the future requires reconstructed people.

The subtitle of Jim Scott's book is *How Certain Schemes to Improve the Human Condition Have Failed.* He begins it, innocuously enough, with forestry: how "scientific" methods of cultivation began to be applied in late eighteenth-century Europe, with the planting of only certain kinds of trees in straight rows, the clearing out of underbrush, and the eventual harvesting of logs that were supposed to be of much the same size, shape, and weight. They were for a while, but over several decades the yield in these forests began to decline. The reason, of course, was that their ecosystem had been disrupted: the bees, birds, and insects that distributed pollen had fewer places in which to nest, the diverse vegetation that had limited the damage from diseases and pests was no longer present, and the effects of windstorms and fires were now more devastating than before. Efforts to make the forest *legible* and therefore *manipulable* had come close to wiping it out.[20]

Scott uses this example as a parable for what he calls "high modernism," which he defines as "a strong, one might even say muscle-bound, version of the self-confidence about . . . the expansion of production, the growing satisfaction of human needs, the mastery of nature (including human nature), and, above all, the rational design of social order [that is] commensurate with the scientific understanding of natural laws."[21] In short, one gives greater weight to general principles than to particular circumstances; one seeks legibility while neglecting accountability; one prefers straight lines intersecting at ninety-degree angles to the irregularities and asymmetries of the natural landscape.

High modernism can manifest itself in architecture with faceless buildings that efface their own inhabitants, or in the urban planning that produces people-unfriendly places like Brasilia or Chandigarh, or in transportation schemes that allow the motorways connecting cities to obliterate neighborhoods and small towns, or in compulsory resettlement schemes like those attempted in Tanzania and Ethiopia in the 1970s, or in such massive rearrangements of landscapes as the New Deal's Tennessee Valley Authority, or Khrushchev's Virgin Lands Project, or China's impending inundation of the Yangtze's great gorges. And, most devastatingly, high modernism can involve the attempted reconstruction of an entire people: Hitler's purely Aryan Third Reich, for example, or Stalin's forced proletarianization of the Russian peasantry, or the most devastating single atrocity of the twentieth century in terms of the deaths it produced—some thirty million—Mao Zedong's Great Leap Forward.[22]

Now, obviously it's a stretch to lump all of these examples together. The human costs of architectural blunders do not begin to compare with the price authoritarian blunders or worse have inflicted upon our era. But remember how often the subject has come up, in this book, of *self-similarity across scale*. Scott doesn't use that term, but I think it's what he has in mind when he stresses the most distinctive feature of high modernism: the attempt to make not just a landscape and its people legible, but their future as well. It's a pattern that persists across vast differences in scale; and what's most striking about it is that such acts of oppression are almost always justified as acts of liberation. Slavery, in this Orwellian sense, really is supposed to produce freedom.

IV.

But of course it doesn't. If, then, the burden of history can weigh this heavily upon the present and the future, then surely part of the historian's task is to try to lift that burden: to show that, because most forms of oppression have been constructed, they can be deconstructed; to demonstrate that what is was not always so in the past and therefore need not be so in the future. The historian must be, in this sense, a social critic; for it's by means of such criticism that the past liberates even as it oppresses the present and future—very much as the historian, however paradoxically, simultaneously performs both acts upon the past itself.

To see what I mean by the past liberating the present, begin with an all too frequent micro-situation: a young person growing up with a sense that she or he is in some way "different." It doesn't matter which way: it could be racial or ethnic status, sexual orientation, economic or social standing—you name it. The constant would be a feeling of isolation, of being alone in a crowd, of not being one of "them." And the fact that kids can be so cruel to one another—to say nothing of what adults can do to kids—doesn't make bearing this loneliness any easier.

Then imagine the sense of relief that comes from learning that you're not in fact alone: that others across time and space have had similar experiences, and that the very criteria that mark you as "different" may not in fact always have been there. Consider the effect of reading, say, Michel Foucault or John Boswell on any young person who is absolutely convinced—as many start out being—that he or she invented homosexuality. Shift, then, to a wider focus: the response within the American civil rights movement when the work of W. E. B. Du Bois on slavery and Reconstruction was resurrected, or when C. Vann Woodward showed that segregation in the South had not always been present. Then expand the view still more widely to take in the women's history movement as it developed during the 1970s and 1980s: the aim here was nothing less than to liberate all women by demonstrating that the sources of their oppression were time-bound rather than timeless.

In each of these instances, learning about the past liberates the learner from oppressions earlier constructions of the past have imposed upon them. "Nothing could be less true than the old bromide that what you don't know doesn't hurt you," Joyce Appleby, Lynn Hunt, and Margaret Jacob have argued. "The very opposite seems more the case."[23]

Of course there are risks in this kind of historical writing. The passion with which you make the case can, at times, overtake the patience needed to establish the case, and a consensus on specific details may or may not be achieved. All of the historians I've mentioned here have been criticized for "advocacy": for letting the cause affect their conclusions. Some have revised their findings; sometimes other historians have done that for them. The basic message, though—that the sources of oppression are lodged in time and are not independent of time—has survived scholarly scrutiny, which makes its liberating effects all the more powerful.

The past, therefore, can free us, just as it constrains us. But there's something of an asymmetry here, for while historians have often collaborated in imposing these constraints, they could hardly have accomplished that without the far more powerful assistance of the state in particular and society in general. Historians are relatively minor actors, therefore, in the coercive process. When it comes to the past liberating the present, though, the role of historians is far from minor: they are these days in the vanguard of the movement, and we have advocacy—the increasing acceptance of the view that the historian *should* make moral judgments—to thank for that. That's all to the good, I think, for if there's to be an acceptable bias in the writing and teaching of history, let it tilt toward liberation.

V.

It's here, at last, that we can begin to get some sense of what the study of history is actually for. Borrowing from Geoffrey Elton, I suggested at the beginning of this book that historical consciousness helps to establish human identity: that it's part of what it means to grow up. But I've postponed until now a discussion of that proposition, because it seemed necessary first to establish how historians think before we could usefully approach the purpose of their thinking. That purpose is, I now want to argue, *to achieve the optimal balance, first within ourselves but then within society, between the polarities of oppression and liberation*.

Go back to the newborn infant I wrote about in the first chapter. It is, in one sense, totally oppressed, as a result of having come into the world totally dependent. But it's also totally liberated, in the sense of having no preconceptions, no inhibitions, no concern for anyone other than itself. We start life, thus, at the extremes, and we gradually narrow the gap between them. As we grow physically we're better able to take care of ourselves, so that we gradually become more independent. As that happens, though, we're increasingly enmeshed within a web of experience, lessons, obligations, and responsibilities. By the time we've become adults, most of us have learned at least to balance these tensions, if not to resolve them.

What would it be like, though, to reach adulthood without having achieved that balance? At the oppressed end of the spectrum, we could come to resemble Woody Allen's movie character Zelig, a personality so malleable, so eager to please, so *legible* that he begins to assume the identities, even the appearances, of the stronger personalities around him.[24] At the liberated end might be the severely afflicted amnesiac Dr. Oliver Sacks describes in one of his clinical essays, whose memory extends back only about two minutes. He's free from all constraints; but because his environment is constantly unfamiliar to him it's also terrifying. "What sort of a life (if any), what sort of a world, what sort of a self," Sacks writes, "can be preserved in a man who has lost the greater part of his memory and, with this, his past, and his moorings in time?"[25]

The irony here is that total oppression and total liberation—if we can take these examples as symbolizing them—both lead back to something like slavery. Freedom comes only from the tension between these opposites. That's why a healthy personality is like Jim Scott's healthy forest. There are plenty of big, productive, and harvestable trees, but there's also lots of underbrush lying around, inhabited by ants, bees, birds, and even parasites. There's a balance between universal knowledge and particular experience, between dependency and autonomy, between legibility and privacy. There's little room here for a belief in independent variables, or in the superiority of reductionism as a mode of inquiry. Rather, everything is interdependent: *personality becomes ecology*. It's what we mean by being well-rounded. It's what it takes to keep us sane.

There's nothing automatic about that process, though, because we've had both parents and teachers to help us along the way. And surely I don't have to stress the extent to which these mentors combine oppression and liberation as they instruct us. They lay out the grids within which we become free to lead our lives. They require some sense of the past in order to do this, but it need not extend back very far. Plenty of people who've known little about history have excelled in preparing their young for adulthood. Plenty of historical illiterates have been impressively literate in other ways.

But what about society, and the role of the individual within it? Just as a balance between oppression and liberation constructs identity for a person, so the same may be true of a social system. Here you can hardly do without history as a discipline, because it's the means by which a culture sees beyond the limits of its own senses. It's the basis, across time, space, and scale, for a wider view. A collective historical consciousness, therefore, may be as much a prerequisite for a healthy well-rounded society as is the proper ecological balance for a healthy forest and a healthy planet.

This is, moreover, something we can no longer take for granted. For disruptions of the balance between oppression and liberation became far greater in the twentieth century than they'd ever been before. Restoring and maintaining that equilibrium, therefore, is a skill to be learned, not assumed. And learning from experience in this instance means realizing that we can't continue to learn casually or haphazardly. This gets us around to the single most important thing any historian has to do, whether in the classroom or in scholarly monographs or even as a television talking head, which is to *teach*.

What you hope for, as a result of such teaching, is a present and future upon which the past rests gracefully, rather as it does within the city of Oxford. I mean by this a society prepared to respect the past while holding it accountable, a society less given to uprooting than to retrofitting, a society that values a moral sense over moral insensibility. Historical consciousness may not be the only way to build such a society; but just as, within the realm of nonreflexive entities, the scientific method has shown itself more capable than other modes of inquiry in commanding the widest possible consensus, so the historical method may occupy a similarly advantageous position when it comes to human affairs.

VI.

I want to conclude, now, by letting my final metaphor go back to my first one, which means returning to Caspar David Friedrich's wanderer and Gwyneth Paltrow's Viola, those backsides so intriguingly turned toward us. I've led you to believe all this time that it's we in the present who are contemplating them as they contemplate the past—or, as I've called it, the landscape of history. But what if we've got that wrong, and they're actually facing the future? The fog, the mist, the unfathomability, could be much the same in either direction. What would be the basis, though, for thinking this the case?

It has to do with teaching, which is inherently a forward-facing activity. I'd define it as the simultaneous oppression and liberation of the young by the old, but also of the old by the young. If that sounds confusing—if it leaves you wondering who's really facing in which direction, or perhaps even a little turned around—then that's my intent, for these ambiguities come with the profession.

We teachers are certainly oppressing our students when we expect them to show up for class, or put them through repeated drafts of their papers, or try to get them to see—this is a particularly difficult problem at Yale—that the grade of A- is not in fact likely to ruin their lives and might even spur them on to greater achievement. But we're also liberating our students by laying out grids, by equipping them with instruments of legibility, and by setting them ashore—as we ultimately must—on some uncharted continent of the mind which it will be up to them to explore.

Almost as important, though, is the fact that our students are simultaneously oppressing and liberating us. It can be frustrating to read the prose of students who consistently—at times, it even seems, conspiratorially—relish the passive voice, the split infinitive, the vacuum cleaner paragraph. It can be dreary to wait for them not to appear during office hours, or to write their urgently required letters of recommendation, or to respond to their e-mails in the middle of the night.

But this sense of oppression quickly fades, when set against the extent to which our students liberate us. They free us, first, from at least some of the ravages of aging: the privilege of professing to the perpetually young is not a bad way to try to stay that way yourself. They also release us, if they're good students and we're good teachers, from our own pomposity: to teach without being talked back to is, I think, not to teach at all. They certainly inform and eventually instruct us: the most gratifying single moment in teaching comes, for me at least, with the realization that my student now knows more about a particular subject than I do. And of course, in the end, our students liberate us from oblivion: they may secretly wish from time to time to have Professor X's head to kick around, like Oliver Cromwell's, but they won't soon forget Professor X.

So are my symbolic figures facing backward or forward? Is it the landscape of the past or of the future that they see? I'm going to fudge that issue and say it's both—that we need not decide—for if we can live with the tension between oppression and liberation in our daily lives, then surely we can live with the possibility that the backsides we see conceal a frontside facing either a past or a future: in whichever direction they, and we, think wisdom, maturity, the love of life and a life of love, may lie.

NOTES

Preface

1 *We Now Know: Rethinking Cold War History* (New York: Oxford University Press, 1997).

2 Miguel de Cervantes, *Don Quixote de la Mancha*, trans. Charles Jarvis (New York: Oxford University Press, 1992), p. 23.

3 Two who have noticed—not surprisingly given the breadth of their interests—are William H. McNeill, "Mythistory, or Truth, Myth, History, and Historians," *American Historical Review* 91 (February 1986), 1–10, "History and the Scientific World View," *History and Theory* 37 (February 1998), 1–13, and "Passing Strange: The Convergence of Evolutionary Science with Scientific History," *ibid.* 40 (February 2001), 1–15; and Niall Ferguson, "Virtual History: Towards a 'Chaotic' Theory of the Past," in *Virtual History: Alternatives and Counterfactuals,* ed. Ferguson (New York: Basic Books, 1999), pp. 71–79. See also *History and Theory* 38 (December 1999), a special issue on the convergence of evolutionary science and history.

4 See, for example, Marc Bloch, *The Historian's Craft*, trans. Peter Putnam (Manchester: Manchester University Press, 1992, first published in 1953), pp. 8, 59; and E. H. Carr, *What Is History?* 2d ed. (New York: Penguin, 1987, first published in 1961), pp. 19–20.

5 The closest is probably Richard J. Evans, *In Defence of History* (London: Granta, 1997), but Evans neglects the connection to the physical and biological sciences that Bloch and Carr made.

One: The Landscape of History

1 Paul Johnson, *The Birth of the Modern: World Society, 1815–1830* (New York: HarperCollins, 1991). For his discussion of the painting, see p. 998.

2 John Ziman, *Reliable Knowledge: An Exploration of the Grounds for Belief in Science* (New York: Cambridge University Press, 1978), p. 21. See also the economist Brian Arthur's short history of modern science as metaphor, quoted in M. Mitchell Waldrop, *Complexity: The Emerging Science at the Edge of Order and Chaos* (New York: Simon & Schuster, 1992), pp. 327–30; as well as Stephan Berry, "On the Problem of Laws in Nature and History: A Comparison," *History and Theory* 38 (December 1999), pp. 122, 132.

3 Edward O. Wilson, *Consilience: The Unity of Knowledge* (New York: Knopf, 1998), p. 26. R. G. Collingwood, *The Idea of History* (New York: Oxford University Press, 1956), pp. 95–96, provides a sophisticated defense of the use of metaphor, based on Kantian philosophy.

4 For a comparable artistic metaphor, see Walter Benjamin, *Illuminations*, trans. Harry Zohn (New York: Schocken Books, 1968), p. 257.

5 Connie Willis, *Doomsday Book* (New York: Bantam, 1992); Michael Crichton, *Timelines* (New York: Knopf, 1999).

6 Marc Bloch, *The Historian's Craft*, trans. Peter Putnam (Manchester: Manchester University Press, 1992, first published in 1953), p. 42.

7 Gertrude Stein, *Picasso* (Boston: Beacon Press, 1959), p. 50. See also Gertrude Stein, *Everybody's Autobiography* (Cambridge, Mass.: Exact Change, 1993), pp. 197–98; and, for a similar point about the writings of Garrett Mattingly, R. J. Evans, *In Defence of History* (London: Granta, 1997), pp. 143–44.

8 J. K. Rowling's description of the latter institution in *Harry Potter and the Philosopher's Stone* (London: Bloomsbury, 1997; *Harry Potter and the Sorceror's Stone* [New York: Scholastic, 1998] in the United States) will resonate with students at the first two.

9   G. R. Elton, "Putting the Past Before Us," in *The Vital Past: Writings on the Uses of History*, ed. Stephen Vaughan (Athens: University of Georgia Press, 1985), p. 42. See also Elton, *The Practice of History* (New York: Crowell, 1967), pp. 145–46; and *Return to Essentials: Some Reflections on the Present State of Historical Study* (Cambridge: Cambridge University Press, 1991), pp. 43–45, 73.

10 Mark Twain, "Was the World Made for Man?" quoted in Stephen Jay Gould, *Wonderful Life: The Burgess Shale and the Nature of History* (New York: Norton, 1989), p. 45.

11 See Stephen Jay Gould, *Time's Arrow, Time's Cycle: Myth and Metaphor in the Discovery of Geologic Time* (Cambridge, Mass.: Harvard University Press, 1987).

12 Niccolò Machiavelli, *The Prince*, trans. Harvey C. Mansfield, 2d ed. (Chicago: University of Chicago Press, 1998), p. 4. Collingwood, *The Idea of History*, pp. 59–60, cites Descartes and Kant on the necessity of displacement for historians.

13 Machiavelli, *The Prince*, pp. 3–4, 22.

14 E. H. Carr, *What Is History?* 2d ed. (New York: Penguin, 1987, first published in 1961), p. 114. See also Collingwood, *The Idea of History*, pp. 333–34. For three recent elaborations on this argument, see Jared Diamond, *Guns, Germs, and Steel: The Fates of Human Societies* (New York: Norton, 1999); Robert Wright, *Non-Zero: The Logic of Human Destiny* (New York: Pantheon, 2000); and, from a methodological point of view, Martin Stuart-Fox, "Evolutionary Theory of History," *History and Theory* 38 (December 1999), 33–51.

15 Jonathan Haslam, *The Vices of Integrity: E. H. Carr, 1892–1982* (New York: Verso, 1999). See also Michael Cox, ed., *E. H. Carr: A Critical Appraisal* (New York: Palgrave, 2000), especially pp. 9–10, 91.

16 For a comparable view of the importance of "consensibility" in science, see Ziman, *Reliable Knowledge*, p. 3.

17 The point is made in Evans, *In Defence of History*, pp. 103–5; Ferguson, "Virtual History," pp. 65–66; and Joyce Appleby, Lynn Hunt, and Margaret Jacob, *Telling the Truth about History* (New York: Norton, 1994), pp. 216–17. See also Bloch, *The Historian's Craft*, pp. 120–22, and Carr, *What Is History?* pp. 73, 82.

18 Machiavelli, *The Prince*, pp. 40–41.

19 *Ibid.*, pp. 98, 103.

20 Thucydides, *The Peloponnesian War*, trans. Richard Crawley (New York: Random House, 1982), pp. 164–65, 240, 472.

21 *Ibid.*, pp. 13, 180–81, 351.

22 See, on this point, Stephen Kern, *The Culture of Time and Space, 1880–1918* (Cambridge, Mass.: Harvard University Press, 1983), especially pp. 21–24, 87, 119.

23 Collingwood, *The Idea of History*, p. 246. Tracy Chevalier's novel *Girl with a Pearl Earring* (New York: Dutton, 1999) makes the point elegantly with respect to Johannes Vermeer.

24 Michael Frayn provides as clear an explanation as is probably possible for a lay audience in the postscript to his play *Copenhagen* (London: Methuen, 1998), p. 98. See also, within the text of the play, pp. 24 and 67–68, as well as Collingwood, *The Idea of History*, p. 141; and for the problem as it relates to the "new" social history, Appleby, Hunt, and Jacob, *Telling the Truth about History*, pp. 158, 223.

25 Harold Bloom, *Shakespeare: The Invention of the Human* (New York: Penguin Putnam, 1998).

Two: Time and Space

1 "To his coy Mistress," in *Andrew Marvell*, ed. Frank Kermode and Keith Walker (New York: Oxford University Press, 1994), pp. 22–23.

2 A point made with firmness in R. J. Evans, *In Defence of History* (London: Granta, 1997), chs. 3 and 4. See also R. G. Collingwood, *The Idea of History* (New York: Oxford University Press, 1956), pp. 192, 246.

3 Woolf's father was Sir Leslie Stephen, the editor of the *Dictionary of National Biography*. Her complicated attitudes toward him are described well in Hermione Lee, *Virginia Woolf* (London: Chatto & Windus, 1996), pp. 68–74.

4 Virginia Woolf, *Orlando: A Biography* (New York: Harcourt, Brace, 1928), pp. 18, 64, 98, 266–67.

5 Hayden White, *Metahistory: The Historical Imagination in Nineteenth-Century Europe* (Baltimore: Johns Hopkins University Press, 1973), p. 5. See also Collingwood, *The Idea of History*, p. 203.

6   "[W]hat we call history is the mess we call life reduced to some order, pattern and possibly purpose." G. R. Elton, *The Practice of History* (New York: Crowell, 1967), p. 96.

7   For Macaulay's Whiggism, see Hugh Trevor-Roper's introduction to his abridged edition of *The History of England* (New York: Penguin, 1968), pp. 7–13. For Adams, Paul C. Nagel, *Descent from Glory: Four Generations of the John Adams Family* (New York: Oxford University Press, 1983).

8   Jan van Eyck's lost *mappa mundi* apparently did something similar. See Anita Albus, *The Art of Arts: Rediscovering Painting*, trans. Michael Robertson (Berkeley: University of California Press, 2000), pp. 3–7.

9   Thomas Babington Macaulay, *The History of England from the Accession of James II* (New York: Harper & Brothers, 1849), I, 262, 298.

10   Henry Adams, *History of the United States of America during the Administration of Thomas Jefferson* (New York: Library of America, 1986), pp. 7, 11–12.

11   For more on the dangers of time travel, see David Lowenthal, *The Past Is a Foreign Country* (Cambridge: Cambridge University Press, 1985), pp. 28–34.

12   Fernand Braudel, *The Mediterranean and the Mediterranean World in the Age of Philip II*, trans. Sian Reynolds (New York: Harper & Row, 1973).

13   Carlo Ginzburg, *The Cheese and the Worms: The Cosmos of a Sixteenth-Century Miller* (Baltimore: Johns Hopkins University Press, 1992); Jonathan D. Spence, *The Question of Hu* (New York: Vintage, 1989); Laurel Thatcher Ulrich, *A Midwife's Tale: The Life of Martha Ballard, Based on Her Diary, 1785–1812* (New York: Vintage, 1991).

14   E. H. Carr, *What Is History?* 2d ed. (New York: Penguin, 1987), p. 11.

15   Robert Darnton, *The Great Cat Massacre, and Other Episodes in French Cultural History* (New York: Basic Books, 1984). This is no idle speculation, for Darnton has pioneered electronic publishing in the field of history. See David D. Kirkpatrick, "The French Revolution Will Be Webcast," *Lingua Franca* 10 (July–August 2000), 15–16.

16   David Macaulay, *Motel of the Mysteries* (New York: Houghton Mifflin, 1979), makes this point with great wit and imagination, as does Peter Ackroyd, *The Plato Papers: A Prophesy* (New York: Random House, 1999). So too did an exhibit by Katie Maverick McNeal, "Natural History," at the University Museum in Oxford in September 2000.

17   John Keegan, *The Face of Battle* (New York: Viking, 1976), p. 13.

18   Stephen Kern, *The Culture of Time and Space, 1880–1918* (Cambridge, Mass.: Harvard University Press, 1983). See also Peter Stansky, *On or about December 1910: Early Bloomsbury and Its Intimate World* (Cambridge, Mass.: Harvard University Press, 1996).

19   Marc Bloch, *The Historian's Craft*, trans. Peter Putnam (Manchester: Manchester University Press, 1992, first published in 1953), p. 101, makes this point in a slightly different way.

20   William H. McNeill, *Plagues and Peoples* (Garden City, N.Y.: Doubleday, 1976). The book was also a window into the future, appearing before anyone had even heard of AIDS but providing as good an explanation as any of how such a disease could take hold. See especially p. 33.

21   William H. McNeill, *The Pursuit of Power: Technology, Armed Force, and Society since A.D. 1000* (Chicago: University of Chicago Press, 1982), and *Keeping Together in Time: Dance and Drill in Human History* (Cambridge, Mass.: Harvard University Press, 1995).

22   David Hackett Fischer, *Historians' Fallacies: Toward a Logic of Historical Thought* (New York: Harper & Row, 1970), p. 65.

23   I follow here H. W. Brand's explanation, in "Fractal History, or Clio and the Chaotics," *Diplomatic History* 16 (Fall 1992), 495. My thanks to Gagan Sood for bringing set theory to my attention, and for recommending a book in which it is provocatively used, K. N. Chauduri, *Asia before Europe: Economy and Civilisation of the Indian Ocean from the Rise of Islam to 1750* (Cambridge: Cambridge University Press, 1990).

24   Stephen W. Hawking, *A Brief History of Time: From the Big Bang to Black Holes* (New York: Bantam Books, 1988), p. 1.

25   For another way of stating this problem, see Evans, *In Defence of History*, p. 142.

26   There is a useful discussion of this paradox in James Gleick, *Chaos: Making a New Science* (New York: Viking, 1987), pp. 94–96. For a website demonstration covering the Massachusetts coastline, see http://coast.mit.edu/index.html.

27   Joyce Appleby, Lynn Hunt, and Margaret Jacob provide a sympathetic but by no means uncritical evaluation in *Telling the Truth about History* (New York: Oxford University Press, 1994), pp. 198–237. See also Terry Eagleton, *The Illusions of Postmodernism* (Oxford: Blackwell, 1996).

28 Quoted in Chauduri, *Asia before Europe*, p. 92.

29 Bloch, *The Historian's Craft*, p. 23.

30 *The Confessions of St. Augustine*, trans. E. B. Pusey (New York: Barnes & Noble, 1999), p. 269.

31 Quoted in Niall Ferguson, "Virtual History: Towards a 'Chaotic' Theory of the Past," in *Virtual History: Alternatives and Counterfactuals*, ed. Ferguson (New York: Basic Books, 1999), p. 49.

32 Singularities are discussed in Hawking, *A Brief History of Time*, pp. 88–89.

33 See Gleick, *Chaos*, pp. 11–31; also Chapter Five.

34 Scott D. Sagan, *The Limits of Safety: Organizations, Accidents, and Nuclear Weapons* (Princeton: Princeton University Press, 1993), pp. 11–52.

35 For a similar distinction between the past and the future, see Bloch, *The Historian's Craft*, p. 124.

36 I have adapted this from Hawking, *A Brief History of Time*, p. 23.

37 Denis Cosgrove, ed., *Mappings* (London: Reaktion Books, 1999), especially pp. 24–70; also Jeremy Black, *Maps and History: Constructing Images of the Past* (New Haven: Yale University Press, 1997), pp. 1–26.

38 Jorge Luis Borges, *Collected Fictions*, trans. Andrew Hurley (New York: Penguin Books, 1998), p. 325. See also Lewis Carroll's 1893 novel *Sylvie and Bruno Concluded*, in *The Complete Works of Lewis Carroll* (London: Penguin, 1988), pp. 556–57.

39 I draw this point from the useful discussion in Jane Azevedo, *Mapping Reality: An Evolutionary Realist Methodology for the Natural and Social Sciences* (Albany: State University of New York Press, 1997), p. 103. It corresponds, I think, to the much-discussed "level of analysis" problem in political science. See, for example, Martin Hollis and Steve Smith, *Explaining and Understanding International Relations* (Oxford: Oxford University Press, 1990), pp. 7–9; and Michael Nicholson, *Rationality and the Analysis of International Conflict* (Cambridge: Cambridge University Press, 1992), pp. 26–27.

Three: Structure and Process

1 Marc Bloch, *The Historian's Craft*, trans. Peter Putnam (Manchester: Manchester University Press, 1992, first published in 1953), pp. 40, 45. Bloch turned out to be wrong about Ramses, whose well-preserved

mummy is now on display in the Egyptian Museum in Cairo for Egyptologists—and everyone else—to gaze upon. I owe this qualification to Michael Gaddis, who has.

2 John H. Goldthorpe, "The Uses of History in Sociology: Reflections on Some Recent Tendencies," *British Journal of Sociology* 42 (June 1991), 213–14. See also G. R. Elton, *The Practice of History* (New York: Crowell, 1967), pp. 9, 59–61.

3 John McPhee, *Annals of the Former World* (New York: Farrar, Straus & Giroux, 1998), p. 36. McPhee is here paraphrasing the Princeton geologist Kenneth Deffeyes.

4 See Simon Winchester, *The Map That Changed the World: William Smith and the Birth of Modern Geology* (New York: HarperCollins, 2001).

5 E. H. Carr, *What Is History?* 2d ed. (New York: Penguin, 1987), p. 56.

6 Geoffrey Elton isn't much more helpful. "Whether history is an art or a science is a dead issue," he writes. "It is both." *The Practice of History*, p. 5.

7 John Ziman, *Reliable Knowledge: An Exploration of the Grounds for Belief in Science* (New York: Cambridge University Press, 1978), p. 3. See also R. G. Collingwood, *The Idea of History* (New York: Oxford University Press, 1956), p. 9; Joyce Appleby, Lynn Hunt, and Margaret Jacob, *Telling the Truth about History* (New York: Norton, 1994), p. 197; and Edward O. Wilson, *Consilience: The Unity of Knowledge* (New York: Knopf, 1998), p. 53.

8 Stanley Hoffmann, "International Relations: The Long Road to Theory," in *International Relations and Foreign Policy: A Reader in Research and Theory*, ed. James N. Rosenau (New York: Free Press, 1961), p. 429.

9 Carr, *What Is History?* pp. 56–57. For more on this shift in science, see William H. McNeill, "History and the Scientific Worldview," *History and Theory* 37 (February 1998), 1–13; and Ernst Mayr, "Darwin's Influence on Modern Thought," *Scientific American* 283 (July 2000), 79–83.

10 Bloch, *The Historian's Craft*, pp. 14–15.

11 Carr, *What Is History?* p. 72. For the Hegelian origins of this idea, see Collingwood, *The Idea of History*, pp. 210–12; and Appleby, Hunt, and Jacob, *Telling the Truth about History*, pp. 66–71.

12 Ziman, *Reliable Knowledge,* pp. 6–10.

13 The actual number is now 206 billion. I'm indebted to Lloyd N. Trefethen for this information.

14 Collingwood makes a similar argument in *The Idea of History*, p. 249, as does Isaiah Berlin in his essay "The Concept of Scientific History," reprinted in Berlin, *The Proper Study of Mankind: An Anthology of Essays*, ed. Henry Hardy and Roger Hausheer (New York: Farrar, Straus & Giroux, 1998), p. 20.

15 For another way of stating this point, see Niall Ferguson, "Virtual History: Towards a 'Chaotic' Theory of the Past," in *Virtual History: Alternatives and Counterfactuals*, ed. Ferguson (New York: Basic Books, 1999), p. 83.

16 See Stephen Jay Gould, *Time's Arrow, Time's Cycle: Myth and Metaphor in the Discovery of Geological Time* (Cambridge, Mass.: Harvard University Press, 1987), especially the drawings on pp. 60 and 71. Also helpful on this subject is John McPhee, *Basin and Range* (New York: Farrar, Straus, & Giroux, 1980).

17 Stephen Jay Gould's title essay in *The Panda's Thumb: More Reflections in Natural History* (New York: Norton, 1992), makes the case for imperfection as evidence of evolution.

18 Natalie Angier, "A Pearl and a Hodgepodge: Human DNA," *New York Times*, June 27, 2000; Stephen Jay Gould, "Genetic Good News: Complexity and Accidents," *New York Times*, February 20, 2001.

19 Stephen Jay Gould, *Wonderful Life: The Burgess Shale and the Nature of History* (New York: Norton, 1989), provides one of the best explanations of how this is done.

20 Collingwood, *The Idea of History*, pp. 153, 202–4. Collingwood is here drawing on the ideas of Michael Oakeshott and Benedetto Croce.

21 Laurel Thatcher Ulrich, *A Midwife's Tale: The Life of Martha Ballard, Based on Her Diary, 1785–1812* (New York: Random House, 1990).

22 Jared Diamond, *Guns, Germs, and Steel: The Fates of Human Societies* (New York: Norton, 1997).

23 Quoted in Gertrude Himmelfarb, *On Looking into the Abyss: Untimely Thoughts on Culture and Society* (New York: Vintage, 1995), pp. 147–48.

24 The student was Daniel Serviansky. Niall Ferguson makes a similar point in "Virtual History," p. 72.

25 See Jonathan Weiner, *The Beak and the Finch: A Story of Evolution in Our Time* (New York: Knopf, 1994).

26 John Lewis Gaddis, *We Now Know: Rethinking Cold War History* (New York: Oxford University Press, 1997), pp. 266–67.

27   The entire process is best described in Dino A. Brugioni, *Eyeball to Eyeball: The Inside Story of the Cuban Missile Crisis* (New York: Random House, 1991).

28   Gould, *Wonderful Life*, particularly emphasizes the importance of this final point, as of course does Thomas S. Kuhn, *The Structure of Scientific Revolutions*, 3d ed. (Chicago: University of Chicago Press, 1996).

29   Jeremy Black, *Maps and History: Constructing Images of the Past* (New Haven: Yale University Press, 1997), contains many examples. See also James C. Scott, *Seeing Like a State: How Certain Schemes to Improve the Human Condition Have Failed* (New Haven: Yale University Press, 1998), for an illuminating discussion of how states impose ideological grids upon landscapes. I discuss Scott's book more fully in Chapter Eight.

30   Jane Azevedo, *Mapping Reality: An Evolutionary Realist Methodology for the Natural and Social Sciences* (Albany: State University of New York Press, 1997), pp. 110, 112. Azevedo actually uses the term "metatheory" instead of "theory" in the second quote, as a way of distinguishing between the projection and the purposes of a map. For reasons of clarity, I've preferred to stick with her use of that latter term in the first quote.

31   A point strongly endorsed by Bloch and Carr. See *The Historian's Craft*, pp. 53–54, 71, 119, and *What Is History?* pp. 28, 55, 59, 61, 103.

32   See, on the concept of "fitting," Appleby, Hunt, and Jacob, *Telling the Truth about History*, p. 248. Collingwood, *The Idea of History*, p. 242, writes of the historian's conception of the past as "a web of imaginative construction stretched between certain fixed points provided by the statements of his authorities." If the points "are frequent enough and the threads spun from each to the next are constructed with due care, . . . the whole picture is constantly verified by appeal to these data, and runs little risk of losing touch with the reality which it represents." Berlin also discusses this concept of "fitting," in "The Concept of Scientific History," p. 45; but I think he underestimates the extent to which it takes place in science as well as in history.

33   This "tailoring" analogy owes a lot to John le Carré's novel *The Tailor of Panama* (New York: Knopf, 1996); but also something to *The Education of Henry Adams* (Boston: Houghton Mifflin, 1961), pp. xxiii–xxiv.

34   The conference took place at Ohio University in May 1994. For a defense of McNeill's method by three sophisticated social scientists, see

Gary King, Robert O. Keohane, and Sidney Verba, *Designing Social Inquiry: Scientific Inference in Qualitative Research* (Princeton: Princeton University Press, 1994), pp. 46–47. But see also Tom Stoppard's play *Arcadia* (London: Faber & Faber, 1993), p. 46.

35 Ziman, *Reliable Knowledge*, p. 36, emphasis added. Contrast this with Collingwood: "Question and evidence, in history, are correlative. Anything is evidence which enables you to answer your question—the question you are asking now. A sensible question (the only kind of question that a scientifically competent man will ask) is a question which you think you have or are going to have evidence for answering." *The Idea of History*, p. 281.

36 Wilson, *Consilience*, p. 64.

37 William Whewell, *Theory of Scientific Method*, ed. Robert E. Butts (Indianapolis: Hackett, 1989), p. 154. See also Peter Gay, *Style in History* (New York: McGraw-Hill, 1974), pp. 178–79.

38 Wilson, *Consilience*, pp. 10–11.

39 Bloch, *The Historian's Craft*, p. 8.

40 Carr, *What Is History?* p. 20.

41 I have in mind especially Atul Gawande, Stephen Jay Gould, Stephen W. Hawking, Philip Morrison, Sherwin B. Nuland, Steven Weinberg, Edward O. Wilson, and Lewis Thomas.

Four: The Interdependency of Variables

1 Even political scientists whose work strongly suggests *interdependency* continue to make distinctions between independent and dependent variables. See, for example, Robert Jervis, *Systems Effects: Complexity in Political and Social Life* (Princeton: Princeton University Press, 1997), pp. 92–103; and Stephen Van Evera, *Guide to Methods for Students of Political Science* (Ithaca, N.Y.: Cornell University Press, 1997), pp. 10–11.

2 See, for example, Richard Ned Lebow, "Social Science and History: Ranchers versus Farmers?" in *Bridges and Boundaries: Historians, Political Scientists, and the Study of International Relations*, ed. Colin Elman and Miriam Fendius Elman (Cambridge, Mass.: MIT Press, 2001), pp. 123–26.

3 Gary King, Robert O. Keohane, and Sidney Verba, *Designing Social Inquiry: Scientific Inference in Qualitative Research* (Princeton: Princeton

University Press, 1994), p. 123. King, Keohane, and Verba prefer the term "explanatory variables," which they equate with independent variables (p. 77).

4 For the intriguing suggestion that reductionism may not work even in particle physics, see George Johnson, "Challenging Particle Physics as Path to Truth," *New York Times*, December 4, 2001.

5 Stephen Jay Gould, *Wonderful Life: The Burgess Shale and the Nature of History* (New York: Norton, 1989), pp. 278–79, points out that the Harvard University curriculum does seem to assume such a hierarchy. That does not, however, make the claim universally valid.

6 I've used the term "forecasting" instead of "prediction" here because it demands less of the disciplines that practice it. "[A] *forecast* is a statement about unknown phenomena based upon known or accepted generalizations and uncertain conditions ('partial unknowns'), whereas a *prediction* involves the linkage of known or accepted generalizations with certain conditions ('knowns') to yield a statement about unknown phenomena." John R. Freeman and Brian L. Job, "Scientific Forecasts in International Relations: Problems of Definition and Epistemology," *International Studies Quarterly* 23 (March 1979), 117–18.

7 John Ziman, *Reliable Knowledge: An Exploration of the Grounds for Belief in Science* (New York: Cambridge University Press, 1978), pp. 158–59; Dorothy Ross, *The Origins of American Social Science* (New York: Cambridge University Press, 1991), p. 390; Rogers M. Smith, "Science, Non-Science, and Politics," in *The Historic Turn in the Human Sciences*, ed. Terence J. McDonald (Ann Arbor: University of Michigan Press, 1996), pp. 121–23. Such claims have become muted in recent years, to such an extent that the terms "prediction" and "forecasting" appear only rarely in King, Keohane, and Verba, *Designing Social Inquiry*. The authors do note, though (p. 15), that research topics in the social sciences "should be consequential for political, social, or economic life, for understanding something that significantly affects many people's lives, or for understanding and predicting events that might be harmful or beneficial." I've discussed the role of prediction and forecasting more extensively in "International Relations Theory and the End of the Cold War," *International Security* 17 (Winter 1992–93), 6–10.

8   I've borrowed this term from Joseph Fraccia and R. C. Lewontin, "Does Culture Evolve?" *History and Theory* 38 (December 1999), 54.

9   R. G. Collingwood, *The Idea of History* (New York: Oxford University Press, 1956), pp. 84–85, describes this as an eighteenth-century viewpoint.

10 See, on this point, Ross, *The Origins of American Social Science*, pp. 299–300; Peter Novick, *That Noble Dream: The "Objectivity Question" and the American Historical Profession* (New York: Cambridge University Press, 1988), pp. 69–70; and Terence J. McDonald, "Introduction," in *The Historic Turn in the Human Sciences*, ed. T. McDonald, pp. 4–5.

11 Smith, "Science, Non-Science, and Politics," pp. 123–24; also Donald R. Green and Ian Shapiro, *Pathologies of Rational Choice Theory: A Critique of Applications in Political Science* (New Haven: Yale University Press, 1994), pp. 25–26.

12 Collingwood, *The Idea of History*, p. 54.

13 Tom Stoppard, *Arcadia* (London: Faber & Faber, 1993), p. 5.

14 See James Gleick, *Chaos: Making a New Science* (New York: Viking, 1987), p. 41.

15 The best overall critique is Green and Shapiro, *Pathologies of Rational Choice Theory*, especially pp. 1–32. But see also W. Brian Arthur, "Competing Technologies, Increasing Returns, and Lock-in by Historical Events," *Economic Journal* 94 (March 1989), 116–31; Smith, "Science, Non-Science and Politics," especially pp. 132–33; and Paul Omerod, *Butterfly Economics: A New General Theory of Social and Economic Behaviour* (London: Faber & Faber, 1998), especially pp. 11–27, 36, 72. I'll have more to say about rational choice theory in Chapter Seven.

16 Peter Burke, *History and Social Theory* (Cambridge: Polity Press, 1992), pp. 104–9.

17 Michael E. Latham, *Modernization as Ideology: American Social Science and "Nation Building" in the Kennedy Era* (Chapel Hill: University of North Carolina Press, 2000).

18 The most obvious recent example is the peaceful relinquishing of power by communist parties in the former Soviet Union and Eastern Europe. But there are also several interesting American examples, among them the Defense Department's strong resistance, prior to the outbreak of the Korean War, to having its own budget increased, while the State Depart-

ment was strongly advocating that course of action; also the Pentagon's reluctance to endorse the use of military force during the 1980s and 1990s, as against the frequency with which the State Department and other civilian advisers have recommended it.

19   Burke, *History and Social Theory*, pp. 114–15; also, for an example of still controversial physiological findings, Simon LeVay and Dean H. Hamer, "Evidence for a Biological Influence in Male Homosexuality," *Scientific American* 270 (May 1994), 44–49.

20   I've discussed some of the reasons for the latter event in *The United States and the End of the Cold War: Implications, Reconsiderations, Provocations* (New York: Oxford University Press, 1992). For the failure of theory, see Gaddis, "International Relations Theory and the End of the Cold War," pp. 5–58; also Richard Ned Lebow and Thomas Risse-Kappen, eds., *International Relations Theory and the End of the Cold War* (New York: Columbia University Press, 1995).

21   William C. Wohlforth, "A Certain Idea of Science: How International Relations Theory Avoids the New Cold War History," *Journal of Cold War Studies* 1 (Spring 1999), 39–60. See also Colin Elman and Miriam Fendius Elman, "Negotiating International History and Politics," in *Bridges and Boundaries*, ed. Elman and Elman, pp. 18–19; and Andrew Bennett and Alexander L. George, "Case Studies and Process Tracing in History and Political Science: Similar Strokes for Different Foci," *ibid.*, p. 141.

22   Isaiah Berlin, "The Concept of Scientific History," in Berlin, *The Proper Study of Mankind: An Anthology of Essays,* ed. Henry Hardy and Roger Hausheer (New York: Farrar, Straus & Giroux, 1998), pp. 34–35.

23   Green and Shapiro, *Pathologies of Rational Choice Theory*, p. 6. Robert G. Kaiser, "Election Miscalled: Experts Dissect Their (Wrong) Predictions," *International Herald Tribune*, February 10–11, 2001, discusses the efforts of political scientists to explain why their forecasts of a Gore landslide in the 2000 American presidential election went wrong. One of them claims simply that "Gore's vote total should have been much higher than it was." Reality, in short, failed theory.

24   See, on this point, King, Keohane, and Verba, *Designing Social Inquiry*, pp. 10–12. The term "punctuated equilibrium" comes from Stephen Jay

Gould and Niles Eldridge. See Eldridge, *Time Frames: The Evolution of Punctuated Equilibria* (Princeton: Princeton University Press, 1985); also Gould and Eldridge, "Punctuated Equilibrium Comes of Age," *Nature* 366 (November 18, 1993), 223–27.

25 The late Douglas Adams, to be sure, did have an independent variable for the Norwegian coastline. See *The Hitch Hiker's Guide to the Galaxy* (London: Macmillan, 1979), p. 143.

26 Alexander Wendt, *Social Theory of International Politics* (New York: Cambridge University Press, 1999), p. 372. See also William R. Thompson, *Evolutionary Interpretations of World Politics* (New York: Routledge, 2001).

27 Terence J. McDonald, "What We Talk about When We Talk about History: The Conversations of History and Sociology," in *The Historic Turn in the Human Sciences*, ed. T. McDonald, pp. 107–8.

28 Paul Omerod, *Butterfly Economics: A New General Theory of Social and Economic Behavior* (London: Faber & Faber, 1998), surveys these trends.

29 See, in particular, Alexander L. George, "Case Studies and Theory Development: The Method of Structured, Focused Comparison," in *Diplomacy: New Approaches in History, Theory, and Policy*, ed. Paul Gordon Lauren (New York: Free Press, 1979), pp. 43–68; Alexander L. George, *Bridging the Gap: Theory and Practice in Foreign Policy* (Washington: United States Institute of Peace Press, 1993); and Bennett and George, "Case Studies and Process Tracing in History and Political Science," pp. 137–66.

30 Richard J. Evans, *In Defence of History* (London: Granta, 1997), p. 83, makes the point clearly.

31 Carr, *What Is History?* p. 63. For a similar argument, see Collingwood, *The Idea of History*, pp. 194–95.

32 King, Keohane, and Verba, *Designing Social Inquiry*, p. 48.

33 The terms are my own, but they follow the central argument in Clayton Roberts, *The Logic of Historical Explanation* (University Park: Pennsylvania State University Press, 1996). They also parallel Jack S. Levy's distinction between the "idiographic" and "nomothetic" uses of theory, in "Explaining Events and Developing Theories: History, Political Science, and the Analysis of International Relations," in *Bridges and Boundaries*, ed. Elman and Elman, pp. 45–47. Berlin makes a similar distinction in

"The Concept of Scientific History," pp. 27–28; as does Geoffrey Elton in *The Practice of History* (New York: Crowell, 1967), p. 27.

34 John Lewis Gaddis, *We Now Know: Rethinking Cold War History* (New York: Oxford University Press, 1997), pp. 288–91.

35 Collingwood, *The Idea of* History, p. 224. See also Roberts, *The Logic of Historical Explanation*, pp. 1–15; and Stephan Berry, "On the Problem of Laws in Nature and History: A Comparison," *History and Theory* 38 (December 1999), especially pp. 129, 133.

36 For a parallel approach in political science, see the discussion of typological theory in Bennett and George, "Case Studies and Process Tracing in History and Political Science," pp. 156–60.

37 The classic texts are Hans J. Morgenthau, *Politics among Nations: The Struggle for Power and Peace*, 6th ed. (New York: McGraw Hill, 1985, first published in 1948); and George F. Kennan, *American Diplomacy: 1900–1950* (Chicago: University of Chicago Press, 1951), although Kennan would not welcome being described as a theorist.

38 Michael Oakeshott, *Experience and Its Modes* (Cambridge: Cambridge University Press, 1933), p. 128, as quoted in Niall Ferguson, "Virtual History: Towards a 'Chaotic' Theory of the Past," in *Virtual History: Alternatives and Counterfactuals,* ed. N. Ferguson (New York: Basic Books, 1997), pp. 50–51. See also Berlin, "The Concept of Scientific History," pp. 37–38; and Jervis, *Systems Effects*, pp. 10–27. I've benefited here as well from the work of one of my Ohio University graduate students, Jeffrey Woods, "The Web Model of History," a 1994 paper prepared in the Ohio University Contemporary History Institute.

39 I discuss this principle of diminishing relevance in Chapter Six.

40 The example comes from Roberts, *The Logic of Historical Explanation*, pp. 116–17.

41 Trevor Royle, *Crimea: The Great Crimean War, 1854–1856* (London: Little, Brown, 1999), pp. 15–19. For sensitive dependence on initial conditions, see Gleick, *Chaos*, pp. 11–31.

42 Or, to put it in political science terms, we are comfortable with "equifinality." Bennett and George discuss this concept in "Case Studies and Process Tracing in History and Political Science," p. 138.

43 For a good example, see Stephen G. Brooks, "Dueling Realisms," *Inter-*

national Organization 51 (Summer 1997), 465–66, which discusses John Mearsheimer's spectacularly wrong prediction that the Ukrainians would never give up their nuclear weapons.

44 King, Keohane, and Verba, *Designing Social Inquiry*, p. 20, argue that social scientists have become too dependent upon parsimony.

45 Bennett and George, "Case Studies and Process Tracing in History and Political Science," p. 148.

46 Gould, *Wonderful Life*, p. 51. The outcome is, hence, "path dependent." For an explanation of this term, which is also gaining currency among social scientists, see Elman and Elman, "Negotiating International History and Politics," pp. 30–31. An analogy in economics is the phenomenon of "increasing returns," described well in M. Mitchell Waldrop, *Complexity: The Emerging Science at the Edge of Chaos* (New York: Viking, 1992), pp. 15–98. Would the seemingly unimportant alteration Gould cites qualify as an independent variable? Only within the particular path, I think, and only on that particular journey along it. There'd be no assurance that it would work the same way on other paths and other journeys.

47 Here I differ, most respectfully, from the conclusion Isaiah Berlin reaches in "The Concept of Scientific History," especially pp. 56–58.

48 Kenneth N. Waltz, *Theory of International Politics* (New York: Random House, 1979), pp. 161–93.

49 John Lewis Gaddis, *The Long Peace: Inquiries into the History of the Cold War* (New York: Oxford University Press, 1987), especially pp. 219–23.

50 Waltz, *Theory of International Politics*, p. 183. In fairness to Waltz, this forecast was not much more off target than one of my own, which was that "the point at which a great power perceives its decline to be beginning is a perilous one: behavior can become erratic, even desperate, well before physical strength itself has dissipated." *The Long Peace*, p. 244. For another failed forecast, reflecting the influence of Waltz, see John Lewis Gaddis, "How the Cold War Might End," *Atlantic* 260 (November 1987), 88–100.

51 Martin Hollis and Steve Smith, *Explaining and Understanding International Relations* (Oxford: Oxford University Press, 1990), pp. 110–18, provide an effective critique of Waltz.

52 For more on this, see Gaddis, *We Now Know*, pp. 283–84.

53 *Ibid.*, p. 284.

54 Paul W. Schroeder makes a similar point in "History and International Relations Theory: Not Use or Abuse, but Fit or Misfit," *International Security* 22 (Summer 1997), 69; as does Michael Nicholson in *Rationality and the Analysis of International Conflict* (Cambridge: Cambridge University Press, 1992), pp. 27–28.

55 See Sherwin B. Nuland, *How We Live* (New York: Vintage, 1997).

56 Samuel P. Huntington, *The Clash of Civilizations and the Remaking of World Order* (New York: Simon & Schuster, 1996), p. 20. See also Sigmund Freud, *Civilization and Its Discontents*, trans. and ed. James Strachey (New York: Norton, 1961), p. 72.

57 Ziman, *Reliable Knowledge*, p. 3.

58 Smith, "Science, Non-Science, and Politics," p. 124.

59 The dissident "Perestroika" movement within the American Political Science Association has advanced a similar set of claims within that field. See Scott Heller and D. W. Miller, "'Mr. Perestroika' Criticizes Political-Science Journal's Methodological Bias," *Chronicle of Higher Education*, November 17, 2000; D. W. Miller, "Storming the Palace in Political Science," *ibid.*, September 21, 2001; Jacob Blecher, "Forward the Revolution: How One E-Mail Shook Up the Political Science Establishment," *New Journal* [Yale University] 34 (December 2001), 18–23; and Rogers M. Smith, "Putting the Substance Back in Political Science," *Chronicle of Higher Education*, April 5, 2002.

Five: Chaos and Complexity

1 *The Education of Henry Adams: An Autobiography* (Boston: Houghton Mifflin, 1961), pp. 224, 395.

2 The "lumpers" versus "splitters" distinction comes from J. H. Hexter, *On Historians: Reappraisals of Some of the Masters of Modern History* (Cambridge, Mass.: Harvard University Press, 1979), pp. 241–43, although Hexter in turn attributes it to Donald Kagan. Adams's Virgin and Dynamo synthesis is chapter 25 of *The Education*.

3 *The Education of Henry Adams*, pp. 224, 396–98.

4 *Ibid.*, p. 455. See also, on Adams and chaos, N. Katherine Hayles, *Chaos*

Bound: Orderly Disorder in Contemporary Literature and Science (Ithaca, N.Y.: Cornell University Press, 1990), pp. 61–90. For more on Poincaré, see Trinh Xuan Thuan, *Chaos and Harmony: Perspectives on Scientific Revolutions of the Twentieth Century* (Oxford: Oxford University Press, 2001), pp. 75–81. E. H. Carr, too, was impressed with Poincaré. See *What Is History?* 2d ed. (New York: Penguin, 1987, first published in 1961), pp. 58, 90.

5   James Gleick, *Chaos: Making a New Science* (New York: Viking, 1987), pp. 46–47.

6   Tom Stoppard, *Arcadia* (London: Faber & Faber, 1993), pp. 44–46.

7   For more on traffic jams and computer simulations of them, see Per Bak, *How Nature Works: The Science of Self-Organized Criticality* (New York: Oxford University Press, 1997), pp. 192–98; also Stephen Budiansky, "The Physics of Gridlock," *Atlantic Monthly* 283 (December 2000), 20–24.

8   William H. McNeill, "Passing Strange: The Convergence of Evolutionary Science with Scientific History," *History and Theory* 40 (February 2001), 2. The point is also made in Niall Ferguson, "Virtual History: Towards a 'Chaotic' Theory of the Past," in *Virtual History: Alternatives and Counterfactuals*, ed. N. Ferguson (New York: Basic Books, 1999), pp. 71–72.

9   Stephen Jay Gould, *Time's Arrow, Time's Cycle: Myth and Metaphor in the Discovery of Geological Time* (Cambridge, Mass.: Harvard University Press, 1987), pp. 120–23.

10 *The Education of Henry Adams*, pp. 226–28.

11 Thomas S. Kuhn, *The Structure of Scientific Revolutions*, 3d ed. (Chicago: University of Chicago Press, 1996).

12 Niles Eldridge, *Time Frames: The Evolution of Punctuated Equilibria* (Princeton: Princeton University Press, 1985); also Stephen Jay Gould and Niles Eldridge, "Punctuated Equilibrium Comes of Age," *Nature* 366 (November 18, 1993), 223–27.

13 Walter Alvarez and Frank Asaro, "What Caused the Mass Extinction? An Extraterrestrial Impact," *Scientific American* 263 (October 1990), 78–84.

14 For a similar but more restrained argument, see John Ziman, *Real Science: What It Is, and What It Means* (Cambridge: Cambridge University Press, 2000), pp. 56–58; also Stephan Berry, "On the Problem of Laws in Nature and History: A Comparison," *History and Theory* 38 (December 1999), 124.

15   As Gary David Shaw has written, "any significant agreement on the terms of discussion [between evolutionary scientists and historians] could give history a more portable language of comparison and analysis than it currently has." "The Return of Science," *History and Theory* 38 (December 1999), 8.

16   Lorenz's experiment is described in Gleick, *Chaos*, pp. 9–31.

17   David Hackett Fischer, *Historians' Fallacies: Toward a Logic of Historical Thought* (New York: Harper & Row, 1970), p. 174.

18   Bak, *How Nature Works*, pp. 49–84.

19   Stoppard makes a similar point in *Arcadia*, p. 48.

20   These and other examples are discussed in Mark Buchanan, *Ubiquity: The Science of History; or, Why the World Is Simpler than We Think* (London: Weidenfeld & Nicolson, 2000). See also Berry, "On the Problem of Laws in Nature and History," pp. 126–28.

21   Stephen Jay Gould, *Wonderful Life: The Burgess Shale and the Nature of History* (New York: Norton, 1989), p. 277.

22   For more on path dependency, see Colin Elman and Miriam Fendius Elman, "Negotiating International History and Politics," in *Bridges and Boundaries: Historians, Political Scientists, and the Study of International Relations*, ed. Elman and Elman (Cambridge, Mass.: MIT Press, 2001), pp. 30–31.

23   Paul A. David, "Clio and the Economics of QWERTY," *American Economic Review* 75 (May 1985), 332–37; W. Brian Arthur, "Competing Technologies, Increasing Returns, and Lock-in by Historical Events," *Economic Journal* 99 (March 1989), 116–31. See also, for an extensive discussion of Arthur's work, M. Mitchell Waldrop, *Complexity: The Emerging Science at the Edge of Chaos* (New York: Simon & Schuster, 1992), pp. 15–98.

24   Robert D. Putnam, with Robert Leonardi and Raffaella Y. Nanetti, *Making Democracy Work: Civic Traditions in Modern Italy* (Princeton: Princeton University Press, 1993).

25   See, on this point, Waldrop, *Complexity*, p. 50. I've discussed these movements more fully in Chapter Four.

26   See Chapter Two.

27   Gleick, *Chaos*, pp. 94–96. See also Bak, *How Nature Works*, pp. 19–21;

Thuan, *Chaos and Harmony*, pp. 108–10; and Benoit Mandelbrot, *Fractal Geometry of Nature* (New York: W. H. Freeman, 1988).

28 Stoppard, *Arcadia*, p. 47.

29 Carr, *What Is History?* pp. 26–27.

30 See Chapter Two.

31 James Miller, *The Passion of Michel Foucault* (New York: Doubleday, 1993), pp. 15–16.

32 *I Shall Bear Witness: The Diaries of Victor Klemperer, 1933–45*, two vols., trans. Martin Chalmers (New York: Random House, 1998–99). See also Stephen Kotkin, *Magnetic Mountain: Stalinism as a Civilization* (Berkeley: University of California Press, 1997); Sheila Fitzpatrick, *Everyday Stalinism: Ordinary Life in Extraordinary Times: Soviet Russia in the 1930s* (New York: Oxford University Press, 1999); and Ian Kershaw, *Hitler, 1936–45: Nemesis* (London: Penguin Press, 2000), especially pp. 233–34, 249–50.

33 On which, see John Naughton, *A Brief History of the Internet: The Origins of the Future* (London: Weidenfeld & Nicolson, 2000).

34 Waldrop, *Complexity*, pp. 286–87. Stephen Jay Gould points out that the tendency by no means exists in all life forms. See his *Full House: The Spread of Excellence from Plato to Darwin* (New York: Harmony Books, 1996), especially p. 197.

35 Kenneth A. Oye, "Explaining Cooperation under Anarchy: Hypotheses and Strategies," in *Cooperation Under Anarchy*, ed. K. Oye (Princeton: Princeton University Press, 1986), pp. 1–2.

36 Gleick, *Chaos*, pp. 53–56, 137–53, 221–29; Thuan, *Chaos and Harmony*, pp. 101–3.

37 Waldrop, *Complexity*, pp. 272–86. See also Stephen Wolfram, *A New Kind of Science* (Champaign, Ill.: Wolfram Media, 2002).

38 John H. Holland, "Complex Adaptive Systems," *Daedalus* 121 (Winter 1992), 17–30.

39 For a methodologically primitive discussion of this issue, see John Lewis Gaddis, *The Long Peace: Inquiries into the History of the Cold War* (New York: Oxford University Press, 1987), pp. 215–45.

40 Buchanan, *Ubiquity*, pp. 37–38.

41 Bak, *How Nature Works*, pp. 1–32; Buchanan, *Ubiquity*, pp. 85–100.

42 *Ibid.*, p. 200. For more on "greatness," see Chapter Seven.

43 Waldrop, *Complexity*, pp. 292–94.
44 McNeill, "History and the Scientific World View," p. 10, emphases in the original.
45 Waldrop, *Complexity*, p. 140.
46 Berry, "On the Problem of Laws in Nature and History," p. 126.
47 A point suggested by Preston King, *Thinking Past a Problem: Essays on the History of Ideas* (London: Frank Cass, 2000), p. 243.
48 For some indications that this adaptation is already taking place in the field of international relations theory, see, in addition to other works cited in this chapter, James N. Rosenau, *Turbulence in World Politics: A Theory of Change and Continuity* (Princeton: Princeton University Press, 1990); Jack Snyder and Robert Jervis, eds., *Coping with Complexity in the International System* (Boulder: Westview Press, 1993); Judith Goldstein and Robert O. Keohane, eds., *Ideas and Foreign Policy: Beliefs, Institutions, and Political Change* (Ithaca, N.Y.: Cornell University Press, 1993); Steven Bernstein, Richard Ned Lebow, Janice Gross Stein, and Steven Weber, "God Gave Physics the Easy Problems: Adapting Social Science to an Unpredictable World," *European Journal of International Relations* 6 (2000), 43–76; and William R. Thompson, *Evolutionary Interpretations of World Politics* (New York: Routledge, 2001).
49 McNeill, "Passing Strange," p. 2.

Six: Causation, Contingency, and Counterfactuals

1 Carole Fink, *Marc Bloch: A Life in History* (New York: Cambridge University Press, 1989), pp. 315–24.
2 R. W. Davies, "From E. H. Carr's Files: Notes Towards a Second Edition of *What Is History?*" in E. H. Carr, *What Is History?* 2d ed. (London: Penguin, 1987, first published in 1961), pp. 163–65.
3 Contrast, for example, Gary King, Robert O. Keohane, and Sidney Verba, *Designing Social Inquiry: Scientific Inference in Qualitative Research* (Princeton: Princeton University Press, 1994), with John Ziman, *Real Science: What It Is, and What It Means* (Cambridge: Cambridge University Press, 2000).
4 The point is well made in Terence J. McDonald, "Introduction," in *The*

Historic Turn in the Social Sciences, ed. T. McDonald (Ann Arbor: University of Michigan Press, 1996), pp. 1–14. It's striking that two of the best recent reassessments of the historical method, Joyce Appleby, Lynn Hunt, and Margaret Jacob, *Telling the Truth about History* (New York: Norton, 1994), and Richard J. Evans, *In Defence of History* (London: Granta, 1997), say nothing at all about the connection between history and the "new" sciences of chaos and complexity.

5　William H. McNeill, "Mythistory, or Truth, Myth, History, and Historians," *American Historical Review* 91 (February 1986), 8.

6　Nor were they alone in using corpses to explain causation. See R. G. Collingwood, *The Idea of History* (New York: Oxford University Press, 1956), pp. 266–82.

7　Carr, *What Is History?* pp. 104–8.

8　Davies, "From E. H. Carr's Files," pp. 169–70.

9　The pattern is documented in Jonathan Haslam, *The Vices of Integrity: E. H. Carr, 1892–1982* (New York: Verso, 1999), especially pp. 59–60, 78–79, 94–95, 128–29, 235, 248; also Michael Cox, "Introduction," in *E. H. Carr: A Critical Appraisal*, ed. M. Cox (New York: Palgrave, 2000), pp. 8–12. See also, for additional critiques of Carr's argument on causation, Appleby, Hunt, and Jacob, *Telling the Truth about History*, p. 304; and Evans, *In Defence of History*, pp. 129–38.

10　Marc Bloch, *The Historian's Craft*, trans. Peter Putnam (Manchester: Manchester University Press, 1992, first published in 1953), pp. 157–58.

11　Clayton Roberts, *The Logic of Historical Explanation* (University Park: Pennsylvania University Press, 1996), p. 108.

12　Carr, *What Is History?* p. 105.

13　Stephan Berry, "On the Problem of Laws in Nature and History: A Comparison," *History and Theory* 38 (December 1999), 122, makes a similar argument.

14　This point is also made in a slightly different way in King, Keohane, and Verba, *Designing Social Inquiry*, p. 87n.

15　See James Gleick, *Chaos: Making a New Science* (New York: Viking, 1987), pp. 11–31.

16　Ibid., pp. 126–28, 160–61; M. Mitchell Waldrop, *Complexity: The Emerging Science at the Edge of Order and Chaos* (New York: Simon & Schuster, 1992), pp. 228–35; Mark Buchanan, *Ubiquity: The Science of History; or, Why the World Is Simpler than We Think* (London: Weidenfeld & Nicolson, 2000), pp. 75–76, 80–81.

17 Waldrop, *Complexity*, pp. 198–240; Stephen Jay Gould, *Wonderful Life: The Burgess Shale and the Nature of History* (New York: Norton, 1989).

18 Gleick, *Chaos*, pp. 16–18.

19 Roberts, *The Logic of Historical Explanation*, p. 111.

20 The best introduction to the theory, which Eldridge developed in collaboration with Stephen Jay Gould, is Niles Eldridge, *Time Frames: The Evolution of Punctuated Equilibria* (Princeton: Princeton University Press, 1985). See also Waldrop, *Complexity*, pp. 308–9.

21 Roberts, *The Logic of Historical Explanation*, pp. 108–9.

22 See, for example, Saburo Ienaga, *The Pacific War, 1931–1945: A Critical Perspective on Japan's Role in World War II* (New York: Pantheon, 1978), pp. 131–33.

23 Are these, then, independent variables? I think not, because phase transitions, punctuations, and exceptional events always have antecedents.

24 Aristotle, *Poetics*, trans. Malcolm Heath (New York: Penguin, 1996), p. 17. See also Anthony Gottlieb, *The Dream of Reason: A History of Western Philosophy from the Greeks to the Renaissance* (London: Allen Lane, 2000), p. 276. I am, of course, indebted to Toni Dorfman for this reference.

25 Bloch, *The Historian's Craft*, p. 103.

26 Niall Ferguson, "Virtual History: Towards a 'Chaotic' Theory of the Past," in *Virtual History: Alternatives and Counterfactuals*, ed. Ferguson (New York: Basic Books, 1997), pp. 1–90, is by far the best defense of counterfactual history.

27 Carr, *What Is History?* pp. 96–99.

28 See King, Keohane, and Verba, *Designing Social Inquiry*, pp. 77–78, 82–83.

29 Although there has been much speculation—and even a 1984 movie, *The Philadelphia Experiment*—about an alleged 1943 teleportation experiment involving the destroyer U.S.S. *Eldridge*. For the Naval Historical Center's debunking, see http://www.history.navy.mil/faqs/faq21-1.htm.

30 One of the better examples is Harry Turtledove, *The Guns of the South* (New York: Ballantine, 1993), which changes the outcome of the American Civil War by giving the Confederates AK-47s.

31 Ferguson, "Virtual History," p. 85.

32 King, Keohane, and Verba, *Designing Social Inquiry*, pp. 82–83, provide a formal explanation of why.

33 The most dramatic recent example is the use of DNA profiling to establish Thomas Jefferson's paternity of one or more of his slave Sally Hemings's children. See the Thomas Jefferson Memorial Foundation *Report of the Research Committee on Thomas Jefferson and Sally Hemings*, January, 2000, at: http://www.monticello.org/plantation/hemings_report.html.

34 L. N. Tolstoy, *War and Peace*, trans. Rosemary Edmonds (London: Penguin, 1982), p. 1341.

35 Collingwood, *The Idea of History*, p. 248.

36 Ziman, *Real Science*, p. 7. Ziman's point here echoes Carr's on history as the inheritance of acquired characteristics. See *What Is History?* pp. 150–51.

37 Appleby, Hunt, and Jacob, *Telling the Truth about History*, p. 171.

38 See Chapter Three.

39 Postmodernist objections to narrative are nicely refuted in Evans, *In Defence of History*, pp. 148–52. See also Appleby, Hunt, and Jacob, *Telling the Truth About History*, pp. 228–37.

40 For parallel arguments, see Collingwood, *The Idea of History*, pp. 110, 240–46; and Appleby, Hunt, and Jacob, *Telling the Truth about History*, pp. 195, 248–50, 259, 268.

41 For a critique of this kind of thinking, see King, Keohane, and Verba, *Designing Social Inquiry*, p. 20. But compare their objections to parsimony here with their apparent endorsement of it on p. 123.

42 Although historians do, surprisingly often, neglect them. See David Hackett Fischer, *Historians' Fallacies: Toward a Logic of Historical Thought* (New York: Harper & Row, 1970).

43 Bloch, *The Historian's Craft*, p. 67.

44 See Chapter Three.

45 For a discussion of documents as a means of reproducibility, see Bloch, *The Historian's Craft*, p. 100. Evans, *In Defence of History*, pp. 116–23, describes one instance in which the footnotes did not hold up; as does Richard J. Evans, *Telling Lies about Hitler: History, the Holocaust and the David Irving Trial* (London: Heineman, 2001).

46 G. R. Elton, *The Practice of History* (New York: Crowell, 1967), pp. 83–87, is helpful on this point.

47 William Whewell, *Theory of Scientific Method*, ed. Robert E. Butts (Indianapolis: Hackett, 1989), p. 153.

48 See Chapter Three.

Seven: Molecules with Minds of Their Own

1 R. G. Collingwood, *The Idea of History* (New York: Oxford University Press, 1956), p. 216, makes much the same point, as does Martin Stuart-Fox, "Evolutionary Theory of History," *History and Theory* 38 (December 1999), 35.

2 M. Mitchell Waldrop, *Complexity: The Emerging Science at the Edge of Order and Chaos* (New York: Simon & Schuster, 1992), pp. 241–43.

3 See, on this point, Michael Taylor, "When Rationality Fails," in *The Rational Choice Controversy: Economic Models of Politics Reconsidered*, ed. Jeffrey Friedman (New Haven: Yale University Press, 1996), pp. 226–27.

4 For a sharp scholarly critique, see Donald P. Green and Ian Shapiro, *Pathologies of Rational Choice Theory: A Critique of Applications in Political Science* (New Haven: Yale University Press, 1994), especially pp. 1–32. Friedman, ed., *The Rational Choice Controversy*, provides a useful forum for both critics and supporters of the Green and Shapiro argument. Less formal criticisms of rational choice appear in Paul Omerod, *Butterfly Economics: A New General Theory of Social and Economic Behaviour* (London: Faber & Faber, 1998); also Jonathan Cohn, "Irrational Exuberance: When Did Political Science Forget about Politics?" *New Republic*, October 25, 1999; Louis Uchitelle, "Some Economists Call Behavior a Key," *New York Times*, February 11, 2001; and Roger Lowenstein, "Exuberance Is Rational," *New York Times Magazine,* February 11, 2001. I should like to thank Alison Alter, Jeremi Suri, and James Fearon for valiantly trying to explain rational choice theory to me.

5 Green and Shapiro, *Pathologies of Rational Choice Theory*, p. 24.

6 See, on this point, Collingwood, *The Idea of History*, pp. 212–13.

7   Barry Unsworth's novel *Losing Nelson* (New York: Doubleday, 1999) is built around the dilemma any biographer faces: that you can never really know your subject. See also A. S. Byatt, *The Biographer's Tale* (London: Chatto & Windus, 2000).

8   There are exceptions to this. Historians like Natalie Zemon Davis, Carlo Ginzburg, and Laurel Thatcher Ulrich have used biographies of "ordinary" individuals to illuminate cultures distant from our own. See, respectively, *The Return of Martin Guerre* (Cambridge, Mass.: Harvard University Press, 1983); *The Cheese and the Worms: The Cosmos of a Sixteenth-Century Miller* (Baltimore: Johns Hopkins University Press, 1992); and *A Midwife's Tale: The Life of Martha Ballard, Based on Her Diary, 1785–1812* (New York: Random House, 1990).

9   David Hackett Fischer, *Historians' Fallacies: Toward a Logic of Historical Thought* (New York: Harper & Row, 1970), p. 49.

10 Plutarch, *Greek Lives*, trans. Robin Waterfield (New York: Oxford University Press, 1998), p. 312. My thanks to Michael Gaddis for this reference.

11 This paragraph is taken from John Lewis Gaddis, "The Tragedy of Cold War History," *Diplomatic History* 17 (Winter 1993), 5–6, which draws in turn from Robert C. Tucker's excellent biography, *Stalin in Power: The Revolution from Above, 1928–1941* (New York: Norton, 1990).

12 Plutarch, *Greek Lives*, p. 312. See also, for a portrayal of Stalin's eyes of which Plutarch would have approved, George F. Kennan, *Memoirs: 1925–1950* (Boston: Atlantic–Little, Brown, 1967), p. 279.

13 For a good discussion, see Joyce Appleby, Lynn Hunt, and Margaret Jacob, *Telling the Truth about History* (New York: Norton, 1994), especially ch. 4.

14 A point made clear in Ian Kershaw's recent biography, *Hitler, 1936–1945: Nemesis* (London: Penguin, 2000).

15 *I Shall Bear Witness: The Diaries of Victor Klemperer, 1933–41* (London: Phoenix, 1999); *To the Bitter End: The Diaries of Victor Klemperer, 1942–45* (London: Phoenix, 2000).

16 Liza Picard, *Restoration London* (London: Phoenix, 1997).

17 For a remarkable identification of a window of opportunity *before* someone jumped through it, see the report of the United States Commission

on National Security/21st Century, which appeared in three installments between September 1999 and March 2001, and is available at http://www.nssg.gov. More widely known for its cochairs, former senators Gary Hart and Warren Rudman, as the Hart-Rudman Report, this study warned explicitly that the United States was vulnerable to highly destructive terrorist attacks on its own soil.

18 Waldrop, *Complexity*, pp. 233–34.

19 Kershaw, *Hitler, 1936–45*, pp. 487, 522. See also Isaiah Berlin, *The Crooked Timber of Humanity: Chapters in the History of Ideas*, ed. Henry Hardy (New York: Random House, 1990), pp. 203–6; also James Q. Wilson, *The Moral Sense* (New York: Free Press, 1993), especially p. 15.

20 A fact that has induced a strange panic among certain historians, as if the barbarians were at the gates. See, for example, G. R. Elton, *Return to Essentials: Some Reflections on the Present State of Historical Study* (Cambridge: Cambridge University Press, 1990); Keith Windshuttle, *The Killing of History: How Literary Critics and Social Theorists Are Murdering Our Past* (New York: Free Press, 1996); and the otherwise admirable Richard J. Evans, *In Defence of History* (London: Granta, 1997).

21 Collingwood, *The Idea of History*, p. 39, also pp. 87 and 199. See, as well, Bloch, *The Historian's Craft*, pp. 118–19.

22 For a recent attempt to deal with these difficulties, see Roger Shattuck, *Candor and Perversion: Literature, Education, and the Arts* (New York: Norton, 1999).

23 John Keay, *The Great Arc: The Dramatic Tale of How India Was Mapped and Everest Was Named* (New York: HarperCollins, 2000).

24 Bloch, *The Historian's Craft*, p. 116.

25 Carr, *What Is History?* pp. 75–79.

26 *Ibid.*, p. 79.

27 Carr to Betty Behrends, February 19, 1966, quoted in Jonathan Haslam, *The Vices of Integrity: E. H. Carr, 1892–1982* (New York: Verso, 1999), p. 235.

28 See, for example, Bloch, *The Historian's Craft*, p. 66; Carr, *What Is History?* p. 120.

Eight: Seeing Like a Historian

1   See Chapter One.

2   James C. Scott, *Seeing Like a State: How Certain Schemes to Improve the Human Condition Have Failed* (New Haven: Yale University Press, 1998).

3   John Prest, "City and University," in *The Illustrated History of Oxford University*, ed. J. Prest (Oxford: Oxford University Press, 1993), p. 1.

4   Scott, *Seeing Like a State*, pp. 2–3.

5   *Ibid.*, pp. 4, 340, 352.

6   Letter from Tom Hamilton-Baillie, January 24, 2001.

7   For a slightly more optimistic view, see G. R. Elton, *The Practice of History* (New York: Crowell, 1967), p. 74.

8   Martin Gilbert, *"Never Despair": Winston S. Churchill, 1945–1965* (London: Heineman, 1988), pp. 1073, 1076–77, 1253.

9   William Taubman recounts the incident in his forthcoming biography of Khrushchev.

10 R. G. Collingwood, *The Idea of History* (New York: Oxford University Press, 1956), p. 141.

11 Ian Kershaw, *Hitler, 1936–1945: Nemesis* (London: Penguin, 2000), pp. 821–22.

12 John Drummond, *Tainted by Experience: A Life in the Arts* (London: Faber & Faber, 2000), p. 51.

13 After which they become, presumably, the grateful dead.

14 Discussed further in Chapter Two.

15 See, on this point, Peter Novick, *That Noble Dream: The "Objectivity Question" and the American Historical Profession* (New York: Cambridge University Press, 1988), pp. 469–521; also, more briefly, Joyce Appleby, Lynn Hunt, and Margaret Jacob, *Telling the Truth about History* (New York: Norton, 1994), pp. 147–51.

16 Collingwood, *The Idea of History*, p. 317. For a particularly good example of a historian liberating the past from retrospectively imposed interpretations, see Joanne B. Freeman, *Affairs of Honor: National Politics in the New Republic* (New Haven: Yale University Press, 2001).

17 Stephen Jay Gould, *The Lying Stones of Marrakech: Penultimate Reflections in Natural History* (New York: Harmony Books, 2000), p. 18. See

also Gould's *Time's Arrow, Time's Cycle: Myth and Metaphor in the Discovery of Geologic Time* (Cambridge, Mass.: Harvard University Press, 1987), p. 27.

18   Stephen Jay Gould, *Wonderful Life: The Burgess Shale and the Nature of History* (New York: Norton, 1989), p. 51. See also Scott, *Seeing Like a State*, p. 390, n. 37.

19   The term comes from Benedict Anderson, *Imagined Communities: Reflections on the Origins and Spread of Nationalism* (New York: Verso, 1991); but see also Eric J. Hobsbawm, *Nations and Nationalism since 1780: Programme, Myth, Reality* (New York: Cambridge University Press, 1993).

20   Scott, *Seeing Like a State*, pp. 11–22.

21   *Ibid.*, p. 4.

22   Scott provides a good discussion of most of these cases. For China's Great Leap Forward, see Jasper Becker, *Hungry Ghosts: Mao's Secret Famine* (New York: Free Press, 1997).

23   Appleby, Hunt, and Jacob, *Telling the Truth about History*, p. 307.

24   This 1983 film contains a little-known cameo appearance by my Yale colleague John Morton Blum.

25   Oliver Sacks, *The Man Who Mistook His Wife for a Hat and Other Clinical Tales* (New York: Summit Books, 1985), p. 23.

INDEX

NOTE: Page numbers in *italics* indicate photographs or illustrations.